1973

The Merrill Studies
in
The Portrait of a Lady

This book may be kept

Compiled by

Lyall H. Powers
University of Michigan

Charles E. Merrill Publishing Company
A Bell & Howell Company
Columbus, Ohio

CHARLES E. MERRILL STUDIES

Under the General Editorship of
Matthew J. Bruccoli and Joseph Katz

ISBN: 0-675-09357-0

Library of Congress Catalog Number: 75-116607

1 2 3 4 5 6 7 8 9 10 — 79 78 77 76 75 74 73 72 71 70

Printed in the United States of America

Preface

The Portrait of a Lady occupies an important place in the cannon of Henry James's fiction. James himself considered it one of his two best — second only to *The Ambassadors*, published a quarter century later—and critics have come to agree with James's opinion. What is more striking, however, is the fact that James knew from the beginning that *The Portrait* was something special, something extraordinary. It began its serial publication in October of 1880, in *Macmillan's Magazine* in England, and a month later in the *Atlantic* in America; book publication followed in 1881. By this time James had published some three dozen pieces of short fiction and three novels, *Watch and Ward* (1874), *Roderick Hudson* (1876), and *The American* (1877). Having served his apprenticeship as a writer, James was now doing quality journeyman work.

As early as the summer of 1877, a few months after he had *The American* off his hands, James was at work on a new novel, one which he felt from the outset would be of another quality. In March of 1878 he wrote to his mother to make an important distinction between two of his unpublished works: "The story Howells is about to publish [*The Europeans* in the *Atlantic*] is *by no means* the one of which I wrote you last summer that it would be to *The American* 'as wine unto water.' *That* is still in my hands; but I hope to do something with it this summer." He adds, a few lines later, that this "is the one that will cover you with fame." The tone, certainly, is jocular, but James was quite serious. The novel in question is *The Portrait* and James saw it as his masterpiece, the work which would earn him a place among the masters of prose fiction — Balzac and Hawthorne, as well as his contemporaries George Eliot and Ivan Turgenev.

The Portrait offered James a brilliant opportunity: it used the international setting which he found so appealing and it featured his favorite character — the American *jeune fille* (as he called her), the youthful and inexperienced young women affronting her destiny in the sophisticated old world. The novel employs typical Jamesian themes — the evil of manipulating human beings, the bitter necessity of coming to know the evil of the world without flinching or turning away, the supreme virtue of looking at life steadily and clearly, recognizing evil for what it is and thereby knowing the good. And if it is tragic to recognize that evil is in the world and that one cannot therefore remain in the world and free of evil, then *The Portrait* is tragic. To fail to recognize, however, that Isabel Archer enjoys an important human success in her career (and many critics have so failed) is another tragedy. The novel is structured so as to express some inevitability in Isabel's falling for Osmond — into the clutches of possessive, manipulating evil — but also in her rise to knowledge with the aid of Ralph Touchett's unselfish love; indeed, her career is presented almost as one of salvation. Her decision to return to Osmond, then, is a positive act — a refusal to attempt to turn away from the world (Caspar Goodwood offers an easy and terribly attractive escape!) but a positive claiming of her right to live and to live responsibly. The novel presents a kind of triumph, indeed, as the pieces by Dorothy Van Ghent and Tony Tanner in this collection strongly indicate.

The critical reaction to the novel was mature from the beginning. The first three selections here indicate the critics' serious response to what they immediately recognized as a serious work of art. The pieces by Hay and Scudder would have delighted James in their recognition of the author's conscious interest both in the depiction of the heroine's psyche and in the attempt to remove the omniscient and omnipotent author from the reader's experience. He would also have been pleased at the mention of George Eliot and Turgenev in connection with *The Portrait* — and at Brownell's consideration of James as their peer.

The other seven pieces of criticism have been chosen for their excellence and for the wide spectrum which they collectively represent. They cover the period since the second world war, which has seen a great deal of scholarly and critical activity devoted to James. The essay by Philip Rahv shows the first serious critical attention paid to James's use of the character of his beloved cousin, Mary (Minny) Temple, something of an ideal American heroine. Quentin Anderson and Lotus Snow make further note of Minny's contribution to James's fiction. Other partially biographical studies illustrate James's apparent use of his father's peculiar Swedenborgian philosophy — in Quentin Anderson's piece; and Leon Edel's comment on *The Portrait* shows the ideal combination of the talents of biographer and critic. The excellent criticism of Arnold Kettle, Tony Tanner, and Dorothy Van Ghent emphasize the artistic achievement of Henry James in his early masterpiece.

Such a collection as this is intended not simply to illustrate various critical approaches by reviewers and scholars and critics to one of the great novels in English; it is intended also to offer to the student and general reader some guidance and assistance toward a greater appreciation of James's *The Portrait of a Lady*.

Lyall H. Powers

Contents

John Hay

James's *The Portrait of a Lady*

If there is anything in the motto of "art for art's sake," if the way of doing a thing is, as many claim, of more importance in literature than the thing done, then this last novel of Mr. James needs no justification or apology. No work printed in recent years, on either side the Atlantic or on either side the English Channel, surpasses this in seriousness of intention, in easy scope and mastery of material, in sustained and spontaneous dignity and grace of style, in wit and epigram, and, on the whole, in clear conception and accurate delineation of character. The title was a stumbling-block to many, as the story pursued its leisurely course in *The Atlantic Monthly*,[1] and now that it is finished it is the title which affords to criticism its easiest attack. It is claimed that the heroine is of all the characters the one least clearly painted, least perfectly understood. But it would not be difficult to say that we know as much of her and of her motives as the author chooses for us to

Reprinted from the *New York Tribune,* December 25, 1881, p. 8.
[1][*The Portrait of a Lady* ran serially in the *Atlantic Monthly* from November 1880 to December 1881; and, in England, in *Macmillan's Magazine* from October 1880 to November 1881. — EDITOR.]

1

know, and the interest of the novel comes in great part from the vagueness of our acquaintance with Miss Archer; and after all, when we lay down the book, we cannot deny, if we are candid, that we know as much of the motives which induced her to refuse two gallant gentlemen and to marry a selfish and soulless scoundrel as we do of the impulses which lead our sisters and cousins to similar results. No one can complain of the clearness with which the other characters are drawn. There is hardly a sharper portrait in our literature, and certainly none more delightful, than Ralph Touchett. None who read the opening chapters of the story a year ago can forget the slight shiver of apprehension they felt when Mr. James distinctly announced that Ralph Touchett was clever, and when Lord Warburton declared that "he was never bored when he came to Gardencourt; one gets such uncommonly good talk." It shows a fine arrogance in the most hardened jouster to throw such a challenge as that. It is said that Shakespeare killed Mercutio early in the play where he appears, for fear of being killed by him; but Mr. James evidently has no such fear of his own creations. From the first chapter to the last, Ralph is "clever, witty and charming," as Mr. James tells us in the beginning, with a charm which over-comes the tedium of hopeless illness and the repulsiveness of death. The book is full of living and breathing characters. Mr. Trollope has never drawn a better English nobleman than Lord Warburton, the splendor of whose environment is delicately suggested, never described, and whose manners are painted in a dozen subtle phrases like these: "He had a certain fortunate, brilliant, exceptional look — the air of a happy temperament fertilized by a high civilization — which would have made almost any observer envy him at a venture"; "his English address, in which a vague shyness seemed to offer itself as an element of good breeding; in which the only defect was a difficulty of achieving transitions." The portrait of Osmond is one of those wonderful pictures in which Mr. James excels, drawn entirely from the outside, but as perfect as if his acts and conversa-tions had been supplemented by voluminous pages of soliloquy. His sister the Countess is equally good; so is the dry, practical, caustic Mrs. Touchett; so is the travelling newspaper woman, Miss Stackpole. It is almost worth while, after reading Mr. James's just but unflattering portrait of Henrietta, to look at a novel of Hamilton Aidé in which the same sort of person is introduced — that you may see the difference between the work of a master and that of a bungler. In Aidé's story, "Poet and Peer," the American "lady-correspondent" is characterized merely by the copious use of the word "vurry" for "very," "Amurrican" for "American," a taste for filthy scandal, and a propensity to say "right away" in places where no Yankee would ever expect it. Mr. James's method is altogether different, as will be seen from this brief extract. Miss Stackpole is visiting at the house of an American banker domiciled in England, and is discovered to be writing a letter for her newspaper describing the place and the people. Miss Archer protests:

"I don't think you ought to do that. I don't think you ought to describe the place."

Henrietta gazed at her, as usual. "Why it's just what the people want, and it's a lovely place."

"It's too lovely to be put in the newspapers, and it's not what my uncle wants."

"Don't you believe that!" cried Henrietta. "They are always delighted, afterward."

"My uncle won't be delighted — nor my cousin, either. They will consider it a breach of hospitality."

Miss Stackpole showed no sense of confusion; she simply wiped her pen very neatly, upon an elegant little implement which she kept for the purpose, and put away her manuscript. "Of course if you don't approve, I won't do it; but I sacrifice a beautiful subject."

"There are plenty of other subjects, there are subjects all round you. We will take some drives, and I will show you some charming scenery."

"Scenery is not my department: I always need a human interest. You know I am deeply human, Isabel; I always was," Miss Stackpole rejoined. "I was going to bring in your cousin — the alienated American. There is a great demand just now for the alienated American, and your cousin is a beautiful specimen. I should have handled him severely."

"He would have died of it!" Isabel exclaimed. "Not of severity, but of the publicity."

"Well, I should have liked to kill him a little. And I should have delighted to do your uncle, who seems to me a much nobler type — the American faithful still. He is a grand old man; I don't see how he can object to my paying him honor."

Isabel looked at her companion in much wonderment; it appeared to her so strange that a nature in which she found so much to esteem should exhibit such extraordinary disparities. "My poor Henrietta," she said, "you have no sense of privacy."

Henrietta colored deeply, and for a moment her brilliant eyes were suffused; while Isabel marvelled more than ever at her inconsistency.

"You do me great injustice," said Miss Stackpole, with dignity. "I have never written a word about myself!"

"I am very sure of that; but it seems to me one should be modest for others also!"

"Ah, that is very good!" cried Henrietta, seizing her pen again. "Just let me make a note of it, and I will put it in a letter."

Further on, Henrietta, who is a ferocious patriot — though she ends by a dreadful act of recreancy — is attacking Ralph for not sufficiently loving his country, and for having no regular occupation:

Ralph bespoke her attention for a small Watteau hanging near, which represented a gentleman in a pink doublet and hose and a ruff, leaning against the pedestal of the statue of a nymph in a garden, and playing the guitar to two ladies seated on the grass.

"That's my ideal of a regular occupation," he said.

Miss Stackpole turned to him again, and though her eyes had rested upon the picture, he saw that she had not apprehended the subject. She was thinking of something much more serious.

"I don't see how you can reconcile it to your conscience," she said.

"My dear lady, I have no conscience!"

"Well, I advise you to cultivate one. You will need it the next time you go to America."

"I shall probably never go again."

"Are you ashamed to show yourself?"

Ralph meditated, with a gentle smile.

"I suppose that, if one has no conscience, one has no shame."

"Well, you have got plenty of assurance," Henrietta declared. "Do you consider it right to give up your country?"

"Ah, one doesn't give up one's country any more than one gives up one's grandmother. It's antecedent to choice."

"I suppose that means that you would give it up if you could? What do they think of you over here?"

"They delight in me."

"That's because you truckle to them."

"Ah, set it down a little to my natural charm!" Ralph urged.

In every detail of execution this book shows a greater facility, a richer command of resources than any of its predecessors. The delicate verbal felicities which distinguished the author's earlier works are here found in such abundance that quotation becomes an embarrassing task. The description of Touchett's house in the first chapter is altogether admirable for its completeness and its reserve:

It stood upon a low hill, above the river — the river being the Thames, at some forty miles from London. A long gabled front of red brick, with the complexion of which time and the weather had played all sorts of picturesque tricks, only, however, to improve and refine it, presented itself to the lawn, with its patches of ivy, its clustered chimneys, its windows smothered in creepers. The house had a name and a history; the old gentleman taking his tea would have been delighted to tell you these things: how it had been built under Edward the Sixth, had offered a night's hospitality to the great Elizabeth (whose august person had extended itself upon a huge, magnificent and terribly angular bed which still formed the principal honor of the sleeping apartments), had been a good deal bruised and defaced in Cromwell's wars, and then, under the Restoration, repaired and much enlarged; and how, finally, after having been remodelled and disfigured in the eighteenth century, it had passed into the careful keeping of a shrewd American banker, who had bought it originally because (owing to circumstances too complicated to set forth) it was offered at a great bargain; bought it with much grumbling at its ugliness, its antiquity, its incommodity, and who now, at the end of twenty years, had become conscious of a real aesthetic passion for it, so that he knew all its points, and would tell you just where to stand to see them in combination, and just the hour when the shadows of its various protuberances — which fell so softly upon the warm, weary brickwork — were of the right measure. Besides this, as I have said, he could have counted off most of the successive owners and occupants, several of whom were known to general fame; doing so, however, with an undemonstrative conviction that the latest phase of its destiny was not the least honorable. The front of the house, overlooking that portion of the lawn with which we are concerned, was not the entrance front; this was in quite another quarter. Privacy here reigned supreme, and the wide carpet of turf that covered the level hill-top seemed but the extension of a luxurious interior. The great still oaks and beeches flung down a shade as dense as that of velvet curtains; and the place was furnished, like a room, with cushioned seats, with rich-colored rugs, with the books and papers that lay upon the grass. The river was at some distance; where the ground began to slope, the lawn, properly speaking, ceased. But it was none the less a charming walk down to the water.

Near the close of the book, when the heroine begins to feel that her life has been thrown away, there is another bit of landscape equally remarkable in its way:

The carriage, passing out of the walls of Rome, rolled through narrow lanes, where the wild honeysuckle had begun to tangle itself in the hedges, or waited for her in quiet places where the fields lay near, while she strolled further and further over the flower-freckled turf, or sat on a stone that had once had a use, and gazed through the veil of her personal sadness at the splendid sadness of the scene — at the dense, warm light, the far gradations and soft confusions of color, the motionless shepherds in lonely attitudes, the hills where the cloud-shadows had the lightness of a blush.

There is hardly a page but has its epigram or its picture well worth quoting and remembering. Some of the most remarkable passages of the book are those in which the author allows the character to draw his own picture, like this — it is Mr. Rosier who speaks, a young American who lives in Paris:

"I like the dear old asphalte. You can't get tired of it — you can't if you try. You think you would, but you wouldn't; there's always something new and fresh. Take the Hotel Drouot now; they sometimes have three and four sales a week. Where can you get such things as you can here? In spite of all they say, I maintain they are cheaper too, if you know the right places. I know plenty of places, but I keep them to myself. I'll tell you, if you like, as a particular favor; only you must not tell anyone else. Don't you go anywhere without asking me first; I want you to promise me that. As a general thing avoid the Boulevards; there is very little to be done on the Boulevards. Speaking conscientiously — *sans blague* — I don't believe anyone knows Paris better than I. You and Mrs. Touchett must come and breakfast with me some day, and I'll show you my things; *je ne vous dis que ça!* There has been a great deal of talk about London of late; it's the fashion to cry up London. But there is nothing in it — you can't do anything in London. No Louis Quinze — nothing of the First Empire; nothing but their eternal Queen Anne. It's good for one's bedroom, Queen Anne — for one's washing-room; but it isn't proper for a *salon*. Do I spend my life at the auctioneer's?" Mr. Rosier pursued, in answer to another question of Isabel's. "Oh, no; I haven't the means. I wish I had. You think I'm a mere trifler; I can tell by the expression of your face — you have got a wonderfully expressive face. I hope you don't mind my saying that; I mean it as a kind of warning. You think I ought to do something, and so do I, so long as you leave it vague. But when you come to the point, you see you have to stop. I can't go home and be a shopkeeper. You think I am very well fitted? Ah, Miss Archer, you overrate me. I can buy very well, but I can't sell; you should see when I sometimes try to get rid of my things. It takes much more ability to make other people buy than to buy yourself.

When I think how clever they must be, the people who make *me*
buy! Ah, no; I couldn't be a shopkeeper. I can't be a doctor, it's a
repulsive business. I can't be a clergyman, I haven't got convictions.
And then I can't pronounce the names right in the Bible. They are
very difficult, in the Old Testament particularly. I can't be a lawyer;
I don't understand — how do you call it? — the American *procédure.*
Is there anything else? There is nothing for a gentleman to do in
America. I should like to be a diplomatist; but American diplomacy
— that is not for gentlemen either. I am sure if you had seen the
last min —"

Of the importance of this volume there can be no question. It
will certainly remain one of the notable books of the time. It is
properly to be compared, not with the light and ephemeral literature of amusement, but with the gravest and most serious works of
imagination which have been devoted to the study of the social
conditions of the age and the moral aspects of our civilization. The
story is of the simplest possible. A young girl richly endowed in
mind, person and character, but with slight knowledge of the
world, unexpectedly receives a great fortune. She has previously
rejected two men of entirely suitable position and qualities, not
because she doubts their worth but because she has certain vague
ideals. She falls into the company of a fascinating woman of forty
who marries her to an old paramour of her own. There is positively
no incident in the book — there is not one word of writing for
writing's sake; there is not a line of meretricious ornament. It is
a sober, consistent study of a single human character, with all its
conditions and environments, in situations not in the least strained
or exceptional. There is nothing exceptional about the book but
the genius of the author, which is now, more than ever before,
beyond question. This simple story is told with every imaginable
accessory of wit, observation, description of nature and of life. But
the reader must take his pleasure as he goes along. He can get
none from the issue of the story, for no one in it really prospers.
The heroine and her ideals come to a sorry market. Even the
wicked are not happy. The little people who furnish the comedy
of the play go out with the half comic despair of children sent
to bed without the toys they had been promised. The nearest
approach to content is the case of Mrs. Touchett, who, after the
deaths of her husband and her only child, reflects "that after all,
such things happened to other people and not to herself. Death
was disagreeable, but in this case it was her son's death, not her

own; she had never flattered herself that her own would be disagreeable to anyone but Mrs. Touchett. She was better off than poor Ralph, who had left all the commodities of life behind him, and indeed all the security; for the worst of dying was, to Mrs. Touchett's mind, that it exposed one to be taken advantage of. For herself, she was on the spot; there was nothing so good as that."

Horace Scudder

From "The Portrait of a Lady and Dr. Breen's Practice"

The Atlantic may fairly claim to have exercised its critical function upon the just completed novels by Mr. James and Mr. Howells before the reader had begun to enjoy them, and to have reserved the right, when the reader should be in full possession, of explaining why and how much it liked them. Yet a book has, after all, a life distinct from the interrupted existence of a magazine serial, and it is quite possible to take up these comely volumes and receive a new impression of the integrity of the stories which they contain. Possibly, Mr. James's novel suffers less than some others might from being read in fragmentary form, for the minute finish of touch with which the lines in the portrait are applied meets the reader's eye with new power every time that he takes up the story after a fall upon other work; yet this very refinement of manipulation may lead one to overlook the larger consistency of the whole figure. It is worth while to step back a few paces, and fail for a moment to see each individual stroke of the brush.

Come, then, since we have been looking at the portrait of Isabel from the near point of monthly chapters, let us seat ourselves

Reprinted from the *Atlantic Monthly*, XLIX (January 1882), 126-130.

before the book, and, armed with an imaginative tin opera-glass to shut out all other pictures, renew our acquaintance with the portrait. How does it strike us as a whole? What is the impression finally left upon our minds? Have we added to our dream of fair women?

The artist gives us this advantage, that all the elaboration of his work looks distinctly to the perfection of the central figure. One can repeat almost in a single breath the incidental story of the book. That is dissolved immediately, if the incidents deposited are the critical ones of Isabel's meeting with her aunt, her rejection successively of Goodwood and Lord Warburton, her accession to wealth, her marriage with Osmond, her temporary separation, and her final return. A person hearing the narrative might be pardoned if he failed to see the making of a great novel in it, but only when one has recited it does he become aware how each step in the fatal series is a movement in the direction of destiny. By a fine concentration of attention upon the heroine, Mr. James impresses us with her importance, and the other characters, involved as they are with her life, fall back into secondary positions. It is much to have seized and held firmly so elusive a conception, and our admiration is increased when reflection shows that, individual as Isabel is in the painting, one may fairly take her as representative of womanly life today. The fine purpose of her freedom, the resolution with which she seeks to be the maker of her destiny, the subtle weakness into which all this betrays her, the apparent helplessness of her ultimate position, and the conjectured escape only through patient forbearance, — what are all these, if not attributes of womanly life expended under current conditions?

The consistency of the work is observable under another aspect. Mr. James's method is sufficiently well known, and since he has made it his own the critic may better accept it and measure it than complain of it. What renders it distinct from, say, Thackeray's method, with which it has been compared, or from George Eliot's, is the limitation of the favorite generalizations and analyses. If the reader will attend, he will see that these take place quite exclusively within the boundaries of the story and characters. That is to say, when the people in the book stop acting or speaking, it is to give to the novelist an opportunity, not to indulge in general reflections, having application to all sorts and conditions of men, of whom his *dramatis personæ* are but a part, — he has no desire to share humanity with them, — but to make acute reflections upon these particular people, and to explain more thoroughly than their words and acts can the motives which lie behind. We may, on general grounds, doubt the self-confidence or power of a novelist who feels this part of his performance to be essential, but there can be no doubt that Mr. James's method is a part of that concentration of mind which results in a singular consistency.

Yet all this carries an intimation of what is curiously noticeable in his work. It is consistent, but the consistency is with itself. Within the boundaries of the novel the logic of character and events is close and firm. We say this after due reflection upon the latest pages. There can be little doubt that the novelist suffers more in the reader's judgment from a false or ineffective scene at the close of his story than he gains from many felicitous strokes in the earlier development of plot or character. The impatient, undiscriminating objection, It does not end well, although it may incense the writer, is an ill-formulated expression of the feeling that the creation lacks the final, triumphant touch which gives life; the sixth swan in the story got a stitch-weed shirt, like the rest, but in the hurry of the last moment it lacked a few stitches, and so in the transformation the youngest brother was forced to put up with one arm and to show a wing for the other. Isabel Archer, with her fine horoscope, is an impressive figure, and one follows her in her free flight with so much admiration for her resolution and strong pinions that when she is caught in the meshes of Osmond's net one's indignation is moved, and a noble pity takes the place of frank admiration. But pity can live only in full communion with faith, and we can understand the hesitation which a reader might feel before the somewhat ambiguous passage of Isabel's last interview with Goodwood. The passage, however, admits of a generous construction, and we prefer to take it, and to see in the scene the author's intention of giving a final touch to his delineation of Goodwood's iron but untempered will, Isabel's vanishing dream of happiness, and her acceptance of the destiny which she had unwittingly chosen. We suspect that something of the reader's dissatisfaction at this juncture comes from his dislike of Goodwood, the jack-in-the-box of the story, whose unyielding nature seems somehow outside of all the events.

To return to our point. This self-consistency is a separate thing from any consistency with the world of reality. The characters, the situations, the incidents, are all true to the law of their own being, but that law runs parallel with the law which governs life, instead of being identical with it. In Andersen's quaint story of the Emperor's New Clothes, a little child discovers the unreality of the gossamer dress, and his voice breaks in upon the illusion from the outer world. Something of the same separation from the story, of the same unconscious naturalness of feeling, prompts the criticism that, though these people walk, and sit, and talk, and behave, they are yet in an illusionary world of their own. Only when one is within the charmed circle of the story is he under its spell, and so complete is the isolation of the book that the characters acquire a strange access of reality when they talk about each other. Not only so, but the introversion which now and then takes place deepens the sense of personality. In that masterly passage which occupies the forty-second section, where Isabel enters upon a disclosure of her changed life, the reader seems to be going down as in a diving-bell into the very secrets of her nature.

What is all this but saying that in the process of Mr. James's art the suggestion always seems to come from within, and to work outward? We recognize the people to whom he introduces us, not by any external signs, but by the private information which we have regarding their souls. The smiles which they wear — and one might make an ingenious collection of their variety — do not tell what is beneath the surface, but we know what they mean, because we already have an esoteric knowledge. Mr. James is at great pains to illustrate his characters by their attitudes, their movements, their by-play, yet we carry away but a slight impression of their external appearance; these are not bodily shapes, for the most part, but embodied spirits, who enjoy their materialization for a time, and contribute to a play which goes on upon a stage just a little apart from that great stage where the world's play, with men and women for actors, is carried forward.

• • •

The perfection of Mr. James's art is in its intellectual order, and the precision with which he marshals all incidents and characters; we have hinted at its weakness when we have referred the reader's pleasure to an intellectual glow rather than to a personal warmth of feeling. The imagination which rules governs a somewhat cold world, and gives forth light rather than heat.

• • •

William C. Brownell

From "James's *Portrait of a Lady*"

Mr. James's novel, which caused each number of the *Atlantic Monthly* to be awaited with impatience last year, gains in its complete presentation, and, like most novels of any pretensions, is most readable when read consecutively. Unlike most novels, however, whose fate (and the fortune of whose authors) it is to appear serially, the reason for this does not consist in the condensation which the reader is thus enabled to make in spite of the author, but in the fact that it is a work of art of which the whole is equal to no fewer than all of its parts, and of which there is a certain "tendency," to lose which is to miss one of the main features of the book. In other words, 'The Portrait of a Lady' is an important work, the most important Mr. James has thus far written, and worthy of far more than mere perusal — worthy of study, one is inclined to say. It is in fact a little too important — to express by a paradox the chief criticism to be made upon it — or, at all events, the only impression left by it which is not altogether agreeable. For the first two or three hundred pages one is beguiled

Reprinted from *The Nation*, XXXIV (February 2, 1882), 102-103.

by a kind of entertainment always of a high order — the dissection
of an interesting character by a clever and scrupulous demonstrator.
After that, though it would be misleading to say that the interest
flags — the interest being throughout the book remarkable for its
evenness — the feeling supervenes that to be still entertained
argues a happy aptitude for most serious and "intellectual" delec-
tation. Most persons will recall some experience of the same sensation in first becoming acquainted with undisguisedly philosophical
writings — such as the writings of Emerson or Burke. To others
it may be indicated by saying that it is just the sensation Carlyle
missed in finding the works of George Eliot "dool — just dool."
In America, it is well known, we do not find George Eliot dull,
and it is upon our appetite for this sort of provender that Mr.
James doubtless relies, and undoubtedly does well to rely. Nevertheless, it is possible to feel what Carlyle meant without agreeing
with it; and though maintaining firmly the absorbing interest of
'The Portrait of a Lady,' we are ready to admit that once or twice
we have laid aside the book for a season, with the exhilaration
which Mr. Howells has somewhere observed to be coincident with
giving up a difficult task. One of the happiest of the many happy
remarks made in 'The Portrait of a lady' is in Miss Stackpole's
characterization of her *fiancé:* "He's as clear as glass; there's no
mystery about him. He is not intellectual, but he appreciates intellect. On the other hand, he doesn't exaggerate its claims. *I sometimes think we do in the United States.*" The person of whom this
is said naturally cuts a smaller figure in the novel than the more
complex organizations, in dealing with which Mr. James is most
at home; and it is the inference from this circumstance that we
have in mind. For not only are the simpler though perennial elements of human nature in general eschewed by Mr. James, but
his true distinction — that is to say, his strength and weakness
also — consists in his attempt to dispense with all the ordinary
machinery of the novelist except the study of subtle shades of
character. In other words, his masterpiece, as 'The Portrait of a
Lady' must be called, is not only outside of the category of the
old romance of which 'Tom Jones,' for example, may stand as the
type, but also dispenses with the dramatic movement and passionate interest upon which the later novelists, from Thackeray to
Thomas Hardy, have relied. In a sense, and to a certain extent,
Turgeneff may be said to be Mr. James's master, but even a sketch
or a study by Turgeneff is turbulence itself beside the elaborate

placidity of these 519 pages. This involves the necessity of the utmost care in presenting the material, and accordingly we have that squaring of the elbows and minute painstaking which not only result inevitably in occasional lumbering movement, but which lend the work an air of seeming more important than any book whatever could possibly be; so that it is perhaps fortunate for its popularity (which, by the way, we believe is extraordinary) that we exaggerate the claims of intellect occasionally in the United States.

Even this measure of fault-finding, however, seems a little ungracious, not to say hypercritical, in view of the distinguished success of Mr. James's experiment in applying the development theory to novel-writing, so to speak. We have ourselves followed the succession of his stories since 'Roderick Hudson' appeared with mingled interest and regret, because he has seemed to be getting further and further away from very safe ground, where he was very strong, and into the uncertainties of an unfamiliar region of which it was impossible to tell whether its novelty or its real merit gave it its interest. The elemental characters and dramatic situations of the novel just mentioned were strongly handled, and the work being, comparatively speaking, a youthful one, its promise seemed even greater than its actual qualities. But, almost as if he had been an amateur dipping into another branch of effort after having demonstrated his ability in one, Mr. James immediately abandoned the field of imaginative romance as it is generally understood. He at once made clear his faculty for his new choice, and the field he entered on with 'The American,' and continued with the shorter stories illustrative of American types, became immediately popular. 'Daisy Miller' may almost be said to mark an era in the mental progress of many persons who exaggerate the claims of intellect occasionally; it is wearisome to recall the "discussions" it occasioned in drawing-rooms and in print. There was, to be sure, a Chauvinist view, so to speak, taken of this and its associated sketches, by persons who omitted to perceive that Mr. James had not only made the current mechanical speculations about "the coming American novel" an anachronism, but had also displayed his patriotism and the national genius by inventing a new variety of literature. But naturally Mr. James might be expected to heed rather those of his readers who appreciated and enjoyed his motives and rejoiced in his discovery of romantic sociology. And this seemed his real danger; for though to these readers this reading conveyed a peculiarly refined pleasure, on account both of its novelty and the cleverness of its execution, there was no certainty that this pleasure was not a rather temporary mood, and likely to pass away after the novelty had worn off. Instead, however, of avoiding this danger by a return to the perennially interesting material with which he first dealt, Mr. James has conquered it, *vi et armis*, by a persistence that at one time seemed a little wilful. No one can now pretend, whatever his own literary likes and dislikes may be, that romantic sociology, exploited as Mr. James has shown it capable of being, is not a thoroughly serious field of literature, whose interest is permanent and dignified.

'The Portrait of a Lady' is a modest title, though an apt one. The portrait of the lady in question is indeed the theme of the book, and it is elaborated with a minuteness so great that when finally one begins to find it confusing it becomes evident that the ordinary point of view must be changed, and the last detail awaited — as in a professedly scientific work — before the whole can appear. Miss Isabel Archer is an orphan to whom her aunt gives an opportunity of seeing the world, and to whom her aunt's husband leaves a large fortune, at the instance of his son, who is unselfishly and romantically interested to see what his cousin will make of her life when nothing prevents her from doing as she wishes. The reader at once assumes the position of this young man, and with more or less (less in our own case, we confess) sympathy, watches the progress of the drama which he has set going. At the climax the heroine discovers that she has wrecked her life most miserably. The spiritual transition from the Isabel Archer of Albany to the Mrs. Osmond of Rome is of course accomplished in part by natural disposition and in part by the influence of the numerous characters which surround her. The way in which this influence is exhibited is a marked feature of the book. If George Eliot was the first to make of this important moral phenomenon a distinct study, Mr. James has here, in our opinion quite surpassed her. Any one can judge by comparing the reciprocal effect upon the development of each other's characters of the Lydgates in 'Middlemarch' with that of the Osmonds here. The other characters are treated with a microscopy hardly inferior. Osmond himself is one of the most palpable of those figures in fiction which are to be called subtle. Madame Merle, his former mistress, mother of his child, who makes the marriage between him and his poverty and Isabel and her wealth, and who, up to the climax of the book, is Isabel's ideal, is, if anything, even better done. There is something almost uncanny in the perfection with which these secretive natures are turned inside out for the reader's inspection. As for the heroine, the American girl *par excellence*, it seems as if, scientifically speaking, Mr. James had said the last word on this subject; at any rate till the model herself is still further developed. For example (p. 344): "She never looked so charming as when, in the genial heat of discussion, she received a crushing blow full in the face and brushed it away as a feather." There are pages as good.

It has long been evident that Mr. James's powers of observation are not only remarkably keen, but sleepless as well. But 'The Portrait of a Lady' would not be what it is if it did not possess a *fonds* of moral seriousness, in addition to and underlying its extraordinary interest of purely intellectual curiosity. There is a specific lesson for the American girl in the first place; there are others, more general, which accompany every imaginative work of large importance. That these are nowhere distinctly stated is now nothing new in fiction even of a distinctly moral purpose. But Mr. James has carried suggestiveness in this regard further than any rival novelist, and though, unless one has ears to hear, it is entirely possible to miss the undertone of his book, to an appreciative sense there is something exquisite in the refinement with which it is conveyed. Refinement in this respect cannot be carried too far. In strictly literary matters Mr. James's fastidiousness may be objected to, perhaps, if one chooses; he has carried the method of the essayist into the domain of romance: its light touch, its reliance on suggestiveness, its weakness for indirect statement, its flattering presupposition of the reader's perceptiveness, its low tones, its polish. Upon occasion, where the circumstances really seem to warrant a little fervor, you only get from the author of 'The Portrait of a Lady' irreproachability. Objection to this may easily be carried too far, however; and those who do thus carry it too far, and argue that no people ever spoke and acted with the elegance and precision of the personages here portrayed, must of necessity pay the penalty of ultra-literalness and miss the secret of Mr. James's success. To characterize this secret with adequate fulness would require far more than the space at our disposal; but it may be sufficiently indicated by calling it the imaginative treatment of reality. In this unquestionably lies Mr. James's truly original excellence. 'The Portrait of a Lady' is the most eminent example we have thus far had of realistic art in fiction *à outrance,* because its substance is thoroughly, and at times profoundly, real, and at the same time its presentation is imaginative. On the one hand, wilfulness and fantasticality are avoided, and on the other, prose and flatness. One may even go further, and say that the book succeeds in the difficult problem of combining a scientific value with romantic interest and artistic merit.

Philip Rahv

From "The Heiress of All the Ages"

Henry James is not fully represented in his novels by any one single character, but of his principal heroine it can be said that she makes the most of his vision and dominates his drama of transatlantic relations. This young woman is his favorite American type, appearing in his work time and again under various names and in various situations that can be taken as so many stages in her career. Hence it is in the line of her development that we must study her. Her case involves a principle of growth which is not to be completely grasped until she has assumed her final shape.

This heroine, too, is cast in the role, so generic to James, of the "passionate pilgrim," whose ordinary features are those of the "good American bewildered in presence of the European order." But bewilderment is not a lasting motive in this heroine's conduct; unlike most of her fellow-pilgrims in James's novels, she soon learns how to adjust European attitudes to the needs of her personality. Where she excels is in her capacity to plunge into experience without paying the usual Jamesian penalty for such daring — the pen-

From *Literature and the Sixth Sense*. Copyright © 1969 by Philip Rahv. Reprinted by permission of the publisher, Houghton Mifflin Company.

alty being either the loss of one's moral balance or the recoil into
a state of aggrieved innocence. She responds "magnificently" to
the beauty of the old-world scene even while keeping a tight hold
on her native virtue: the ethical stamina, good will, and inwardness
of her own provincial background. And thus living up to her
author's idea both of Europe and America, she is able to mediate,
if not wholly to resolve, the conflict between the two cultures,
between innocence and experience, between the sectarian code of
the fathers and the more 'civilized' though also more devious and
dangerous code of the lovers. No wonder James commends her
in terms that fairly bristle with heroic intentions and that in the
preface to *The Wings of the Dove* he goes so far as to credit her
with the great historic boon of being "that certain sort of young
American," exceptionally endowed with "liberty of action, of
choice, of appreciation, of contact . . . who is more the 'heir of all
the ages' than any other young person whatsoever."

•   •   •

The initial assignment of this heroine is to reconnoiter the
scene rather than take possession of it. As yet she is not recognized
as the legitimate heiress but merely as a candidate for the inheritance. Such is the part played by Mary Garland, for instance, a
small-town girl from New England who herself feels the pull of
the "great world" even as she tries to save her errant lover from
its perils (*Roderick Hudson*, 1875). Daisy Miller, a young lady
whose friends are distressed by the odd mixture of spontaneous
grace, audacity, and puerility in her deportment, is also cast in
this role, though with somewhat special and limited intentions.
Bessie Alden (*An International Episode*, 1878), a more cultivated
and socially entrenched figure than the famous Daisy, voyages to
England — inevitably so — for the sake of enjoying its picturesque
associations; and she is noteworthy as the first of the James girls
to reap the triumph of turning down the proposal of an old-world
aristocrat. But it is in Isabel Archer *(The Portrait of a Lady)* that
we first encounter this heroine in a truly pivotal position, com-
prising the dramatic consequences of a conflict not merely of manners but of morals as well. In Isabel her heretofore scattered traits
are unified and corrected in the light of James's growing recognition
of the importance of her claims. Two decades later, at the time
when his writing had settled into the so portentously complex style

of his ultimate period, she reappears as the masterful though stricken Milly Theale of *The Wings of the Dove* and as the impeccable Maggie Verver of *The Golden Bowl,* to whom all shall be given.

• • •

As the 1870's come to a close, James is done with the preliminary studies of his heroine. Now he undertakes to place her in a longer narrative — *The Portrait of a Lady* — the setting and action of which are at last commensurate with the "mysterious purposes" and "vast designs" of her character. In the preface to the New York edition (written nearly a quarter of a century later) he recalls that the conception of a "certain young woman affronting her destiny had begun with being all my outfit for the large building of the novel"; and he reports that in its composition he was faced with only one leading question: "What will she 'do'?" But this is mainly a rhetorical question, for naturally "the first thing she'll do will be to come to Europe — which in fact will form, and all inevitably, no small part of her principal adventure." *The Portrait* is by far the best novel of James's early prime, bringing to an end his literary apprenticeship and establishing the norms of his world. Its author has not yet entirely divorced himself from Victorian models in point of structure, and as a stylist he is still mindful of the reader's more obvious pleasure, managing his prose with an eye to outward as well as inward effects. It is a lucid prose, conventional yet free, marked by aphoristic turns of phrase and by a kind of intellectual gaiety in the formulations of ideas. There are few signs as yet of that well-nigh metaphysical elaboration of the sensibility by which he is to become known as one of the foremost innovators in modern writing.

Isabel Archer is a young lady of an Emersonian cast of mind, but her affinity as a fictional character is rather with those heroines of Turgenev in whose nature an extreme tenderness is conjoined with unusual strength of purpose.[1] No sooner does Isabel arrive

---

[1] The influence may well be conscious in this case, though in the preface to the novel James admits to being influenced by the Russian novelist only on the technical plane, with respect to the manner of placing characters in fiction. James's critical essays abound with favorable references to Turgenev, whose friendship he cultivated in Paris and of whom he invariably spoke with enthusiasm.

at the country-house of her uncle Mr. Touchett, an American banker residing in England, than everyone recognizes her for what she is — "a delicate piece of human machinery." Her cousin Ralph questions his mother: "Who is this rare creature, and what is she? Where did you find her?" "I found her," she replies, "in an old house at Albany, sitting in a dreary room on a rainy day. . . . She didn't know she was bored, but when I told her she seemed grateful for the hint. . . . I thought she was meant for something better. It occurred to me it would be a kindness to take her about and introduce her to the world." The American Cinderella thus precipitated from the town of Albany into the "great world" knows exactly what she must look forward to. "To be as happy as possible," she confides in Ralph, "that's what I came to Europe for." It is by no means a simple answer. On a later and more splendid occasion it is to be repeated by Maggie Verver, who proclaims her faith, even as the golden bowl crashes to the ground, in a "happiness without a hole in it . . . the golden bowl as it *was* to have been . . . the bowl with all our happiness in it, the bowl without a crack in it." This is the crowning illusion and pathos, too, of the heiress, that she believes such happiness to be attainable, that money can buy it and her mere good faith can sustain it. And even when eventually her European entanglements open her eyes to the fact that virtue and experience are not so charmingly compatible after all, that the Old World has a fierce energy of its own and that its "tone of time" is often pitched in a sinister key, she still persists in her belief that this same world will yield her a richly personal happiness, proof against the evil spawned by others less fortunate than herself; and this belief is all the more expressive because it is wholly of a piece with the psychology of the heiress as a national type. The ardor of Americans in pursuing happiness as a personal goal is equalled by no other people, and when it eludes them none are so hurt, none so shamed. Happiness, one might say, is really their private equivalent of such ideals as progress and universal justice. They take for granted, with a faith at once deeply innocent and deeply presumptuous, that they deserve nothing less and that to miss it is to miss life itself.

The heiress is not to be humbled by the tests to which life in Europe exposes her. The severer the test the more intense the glow of her spirit. Is she not the child, as Isabel proudly declares, of that "great country which stretches beyond the rivers and across the prairies, blooming and smiling and spreading, till it stops at the blue Pacific! A strong, sweet, fresh odour seems to rise from it. . . ." The Emersonian note is sounded again and again by Isabel. She is truly the Young American so grandly pictured by the Concord idealist in his essay of that title, the Young American bred in a land "offering opportunity to the human mind not known in any other region" and hence possessed of an "organic simplicity and liberty, which, when it loses its balance, redresses itself presently. . . ." Witness the following passage of character-analysis, with its revelation of Isabel's shining beneficient Emersonianism:

> Every now and then Isabel found out she was wrong, and then she treated herself to a week of passionate humility. After that she held her head higher than ever; for it was of no use, she had an unquenchable desire to think well of herself. She had a theory that it was only on this condition that life was worth living: that one should be of the best, should be conscious of a fine organization . . . *should move in a realm of light, of natural wisdom, of happy impulse, of inspiration fully chronic. It was almost as unnecessary to cultivate doubt of oneself as to cultivate doubt of one's best friend.* . . . The girl had a certain nobleness of imagination which rendered her a good many services and played her a good many tricks. She spent half her time in thinking of beauty, and bravery, and magnanimity; *she had a fixed determination to regard the world as a place of brightness, of free expansion, of irresistible action; she thought it would be detestable to be afraid or ashamed.* (Italics not in the original.)

Still more revealing is the exchange between Isabel and the thoroughly Europeanised Madame Merle on the subject of the individual's capacity for self-assertion in the face of outward circumstances:

> Madame Merle: "When you have lived as long as I, you will see that every human being has his shell, that you must take the shell into account. By the shell I mean the whole envelope of circumstances. There is no such thing as an isolated man or woman; we're each of us made up of a cluster of circumstances. What do you call one's self? Where does it begin? Where does it end? It overflows into everything that belongs to me — and then it flows back again. I know that a large part of myself is in the dresses I choose to wear. I have a great respect for *things!*"
> Isabel: "I don't agree with you. . . . I think just the other way. I don't know whether I succeed in expressing myself, but I know that nothing else expresses me. Nothing that belongs to me is a mea-

sure of me; on the contrary, it's a limit, a barrier, and a perfectly arbitrary one."[2]

In *The Portrait* James is still hesitating between the attitude of Madame Merle and that of Isabel, and his irony is provoked by the excessive claims advanced by both sides. But in years to come he is to be drawn more and more to the "European" idea of the human self, his finer discriminations being increasingly engaged by the "envelope of circumstances" in which it is contained.

Isabel is above all a young lady of principles, and her most intimate decisions are ruled by them. In refusing the proposal of the grandiose Lord Warburton, she wonders what ideal aspiration or design upon fate or conception of happiness prompts her to renounce such a chance for glamor and worldly satisfaction. Never had she seen a "personage" before, as there were none in her native land; of marriage she had been acustomed to think solely in terms of character — "of what one likes in a gentleman's mind and in his talk . . . hitherto her visions of a completed life had concerned themselves largely with moral images — things as to which the question would be whether they pleased her soul." But if an aristocratic marriage is not to Isabel's liking, neither is the strictly hometown alternative of marrying a business man. The exemplary Caspar Goodwood, who owns a cotton-mill and is the embodiment of patriotic virtue, likewise fails to win her consent. — "His jaw was too square and grim, and his figure too straight and stiff; these things suggested a want of easy adaptability to some of the occasions of life."

Isabel having so far lacked the requisite fortune to back up her assumption of the role of the heiress, her cousin Ralph provides what is wanting by persuading his dying father to leave her a large sum of money. "I should like to make her rich," Ralph declares. "What do you mean by rich?" "I call people rich when they are able to gratify their imagination." Thus Isabel enters the uppermost circle of her author's hierarchy, the circle of those favored few who, unhampered by any material coercion, are at once free to make what they can of themselves and to accept the fullest moral responsibility for what happens to them in conse-

---

[2]Note the close parallel between Isabel's reply to Madame Merle and the Emersonian text. "You think me the child of my circumstances: I make my circumstances. Let any thought or motive of mine be different from what they are, the difference will transform my condition and economy. . . . You call it the power of circumstance, but it is the power of me" *(The Transcendentalist)*.

quence. Now the stage is set for the essential Jamesian drama of free choice. In this novel, however, the transcendent worth of such freedom is not yet taken for granted as it is in *The Wings of the Dove* and *The Golden Bowl.* There is the intervention, for instance, of the lady-correspondent Henrietta Stackpole, who is no passionate pilgrim but the mouthpiece, rather, of popular Americanism. It is she who questions Isabel's future on the ground that her money will work against her by bolstering her romantic inclinations. Henrietta is little more than a fictional convenience used to furnish the story with comic relief; but at this juncture of the plot she becomes the agent of a profound criticism aimed, in the last analysis, at James himself, at his own tendency to romanticise the values to which privilege lays claim. And what Henrietta has to say is scarcely in keeping with her habitual manner of the prancing female journalist. Characteristically enough, she begins by remarking that she has no fear of Isabel turning into a sensual woman; the peril she fears is of a different nature:

"The peril for you is that you live too much in the world of your own dreams — you are not enough in contact with reality — with the toiling, striving, suffering, I may even say, sinning world that surrounds you. You are too fastidious, you have too many graceful illusions. Your newly-acquired thousands will shut you up more and more in the society of selfish and heartless people, who will be interested in keeping up those illusions. . . . You think, furthermore, that you can lead a romantic life, that you can live by pleasing others and pleasing yourself. You will find you are mistaken. Whatever life you lead, you must put your soul into it — to make any sort of success of it; and from the moment you do that it ceases to be romance, I assure you; it becomes reality! . . . you think we can escape disagreeable duties by taking romantic views — that is your great illusion, my dear."

The case against the snobbish disposition of the Jamesian culture-seekers and their over-estimation of the worldly motive has seldom been so shrewdly and clearly stated. But Isabel is not especially vulnerable to criticism of this sort. It is only in her later incarnations that the heiress succumbs more and more to precisely the illusions of which Henrietta gives warning — so much so that in the end, when Maggie Verver appears on the scene, the life she leads may be designated, from the standpoint of the purely social analyst, as a romance of bourgeois materialism, the American romance of newly-got wealth divesting itself of its plebeian origins in an ectasy of refinement!

Henrietta's words, moreover, are meant to prefigure the tragedy of Isabel's marriage to Gilbert Osmond, an Italianate American, virtually a European, whom she takes to be what he is not — a decent compromise between the moral notions of her American background and the glamor of the European foreground. Osmond, whose special line is a dread of vulgarity, employs a kind of sincere cunning in presenting himself to Isabel as the most fastidious gentleman living, concerned above all with making his life a work of art and resolved, since he could never hope to attain the status he actually deserved, "not to go in for honors." The courtship takes place in Rome and in Florence, where Isabel is swayed by her impression of Osmond as a "quiet, clever, distinguished man, strolling on a moss-grown terrace above the sweet Val d'Arno . . . the picture was not brilliant, but she liked its lowness of tone, and the atmosphere of summer twilight that pervaded it. . . . It seemed to speak of a serious choice, a choice between things of a shallow and things of a deep interest; of a lonely, studious life in a lovely land." But the impression is false. Only when it is too late does she learn that he had married her for her money with the connivance of Madame Merle, his former mistress, who had undertaken to influence her in his behalf. This entrapment of Isabel illustrates a recurrent formula of James's fiction. The person springing the trap is almost invariably driven by mercenary motives, and, like Osmond, is capable of accomplishing his aim by simulating a sympathy and understanding that fascinate the victim and render her (or him) powerless.[3] Osmond still retains some features of the old-fashioned villain, but his successors are gradually freed from the encumbrances of melodrama. Merton Densher *(The Wings of the Dove)* and Prince Amerigo *(The Golden Bowl)* are men of grace and intelligence, whose wicked behavior is primarily determined by the situation in which they find themselves.

Osmond reacts to the Emersonian strain in Isabel as to a personal offence. He accuses her of wilfully rejecting traditional values

---

[3]It seems to me that this brand of evil has much in common with the "unpardonable sin" by which Hawthorne was haunted — the sin of *using* other people, of "violating the sanctity of a human heart." Chillingsworth in *The Scarlet Letter* is essentially this type of sinner, and so is Miriam's model in *The Marble Faun*. In James, however, the evil characters have none of the Gothic *mystique* which is to be found in Hawthorne. Their motives are transparent.

and of harboring sentiments "worthy of a radical newspaper or a Unitarian preacher." And she, on her part, discovers that his fastidiousness reduced itself to a "sovereign contempt for every one but some or three or four exalted people whom he envied, and for everything but half-a-dozen ideas of his own . . . he pointed out to her so much of the baseness and shabbiness of life . . . but this base, ignoble world, it appeared, was after all what one was to live for; one was to keep it forever in one's eye, in order, not to enlighten, or convert, or redeem, but to extract from it some recognition of one's superiority." Isabel's notion of the aristocratic life is "simply the union of great knowledge with great liberty," whereas for Osmond it is altogether a "thing of forms," an attitude of conscious calculation. His esteem for tradition is boundless; if one was so unfortunate as not to be born to an illustrious tradition, then "one must immediately proceed to make it."[4] A sense of darkness and suffocation takes hold of Isabel as her husband's rigid system closes in on her. She believes that there can be no release from the bondage into which she had fallen and that only through heroic suffering is its evil to be redeemed. On this tragic note the story ends.

• • •

---

[4]The significance of Osmond's character has generally been underrated by the critics of James. For quite apart from his more personal traits (such as his depravity, which is a purely novelistic element), he is important as a cultural type in whom the logic of "traditionalism" is developed to its furthest limits. As a national group the American intellectuals suffer from a sense of inferiority toward the past, and this residue of "colonial" feeling is also to be detected in those among them who raise the banner of tradition. It is shown in their one-sided conformity to the idea of tradition, in their readiness to inflate the meanings that may be derived from it. Their tendency is to take literally what their European counterparts are likely to take metaphorically and imaginatively. My idea is that James tried to overcome this bias which he suspected in himself by objectifying it in the portrait of Osmond. To this day, however, the shadow of Gilbert Osmond falls on many a page of American writing whose author — whether critic, learned poet, or academic "humanist" — presents himself, with all the exaggerated zeal and solemnity of a belated convert, as a spokesman of tradition.

Dorothy Van Ghent

On *The Portrait of a Lady*

To go from Hardy's *Tess* to James's *The Portrait of a Lady* is
to go from Stonehenge to St. Peter's and from a frozen northern
turnip field, eyed hungrily by polar birds, to the Cascine gardens
where nightingales sing. Though both books concern the "campaign" of a young woman — a campaign that, expressed most
simply, is a campaign to *live* — a greater difference of atmosphere
could scarcely be imagined nor of articulation of what it means
to live. The gaunt arctic birds in *Tess* have witnessed, with their
"tragical eyes," cataclysms that no human eye might see, but of
which they retain no memory. The birds offer a symbol of Tess's
world: a world inimical to consciousness, where one should have
no memory (Tess's fatal error is to remember her own past), where
the eye of the mind should remain blank, where aesthetic and
moral perceptivity is traumatic. The nightingales that sing to
Isabel Archer and her lover in the "grey Italian shade" also offer
a symbol of a world: they are the very voice of memory, of an
imperishable consciousness at once recreating and transcending its

ancient, all-human knowledge. It is to the tutelage of the European memory that Isabel Archer passionately surrenders herself in her campaign *to live*, that is, to become conscious; for, in James's world, the highest affirmation of life is the development of the subtlest and most various consciousness. In doing so, she must — like the girl in the barbarous legend of the nightingale, who, likewise in a foreign land, read an obscene crime in the weaving of a tapestry — come into knowledge of an evil which, in its own civilized kind, is as corrupting and implacable as that in the old tale. But consciousness here, as an activity nourished by knowledge, transcends the knowledge which is its content: and this too is in analogy with the ancient symbolic tale, where knowledge of evil is transcended, in the very doom of its reiteration, by the bird's immortal song.

The *Portrait* is not, like *Tess*, a tragedy, but it is as deeply informed with the tragic view of life: that tragic view whose essence is contained in the words, "He who loses his life shall find it," and "Except a corn of wheat fall into the ground and die, it abideth alone: but if it die, it bringeth forth much fruit." We associate tragic seriousness of import in a character's destiny with tension between the power of willing (which is "free") and the power of circumstances ("necessity") binding and limiting the will; and if either term of the tension seems lacking, seriousness of import fails. Apparently, no two authors could be at further antipodes than James and Hardy in the respective emphases they place on these terms. In Hardy, the protagonist's volition founders at every move on a universally mechanical, mysteriously hostile necessity; it is only in Tess's last acts, of blood sacrifice and renunciation of life, that her will appallingly asserts its freedom and that she gains her tragic greatness. In James's *Portrait*, and in his other novels as well, the protagonist appears to have an extraordinarily unhampered play of volition. This appearance of extraordinary freedom from the pressure of circumstances is largely due to the "immense deal of money" (the phrase is taken from an early page of *The Portrait*) with which James endows his world — for, in an acquisitive culture, money is the chief symbol of freedom. The vague rich gleams of money are on every cornice and sift through every vista of the world of *The Portrait*, like the muted gold backgrounds of old Persian illuminations; and the human correlative of the money is a type of character fully privileged with easy mobility upon the face of the earth and with magnificent opportunities for the cultivation of aesthetic and intel-

lectual refinements. It is by visualizing with the greatest clarity
the lustrously moneyed tones of the James universe that we make
ourselves able to see the more clearly what grave, somber shapes
of illusion and guilt he organizes in this novel. The tension between
circumstances and volition, "necessity" and "freedom," is demonstrated at the uppermost levels of material opportunity where,
presumably, there is most freedom and where therefore freedom
becomes most threatening — and where necessity wears its most
insidious disguise, the disguise of freedom.

In following the previous studies, the reader will perhaps have
been impressed with the fact that the novel as a genre has shown,
from *Don Quixote* on, a constant concern with the institutions
created by the circulation of money and with the fantasies arising
from the having of it, or, more especially, the not having it; a
concern not always so direct as that of *Moll Flanders* and *Vanity
Fair*, but almost inevitably implicit at least, expressed in indirect
forms of aspiration and encitement to passion. As the definitively
middle-class literary genre, the novel purchased its roots in a
money-conscious social imagination. The wealth shining on the
James world is a kind of apogee of the novel's historical concern
with money, showing itself, in *The Portrait*, as a grandly sweeping
postulate of possession: as if to say, "Here, now, is all the beautiful
money, in the most liberating quantities: what ambition, what
temptation, what errors of the will, what evil, what suffering, what
salvation still denote the proclivities of the human even in a world
so bountifully endowed?"

The "international myth"[1] that operates broadly in James's
work, and that appears, in this novel, in the typical confrontation
of American innocence and moral rigor with the tortuosities of
an older civilization, gives its own and special dimension to the
moneyed prospect. James came to maturity in a post-Civil War
America euphoric with material achievement. In terms of the
Jamesian "myth," American wealth is now able to buy up the
whole museum of Europe, all its visible "point" of art objects
and culture prestige, to take back home and set up in the front
yard (we need look no further, for historical objectification of this
aspect of the "myth," than to William Randolph Hearst's epic
importation of various priceless chunks of Europe to California).

---

[1] Discussion of James's "international myth" will be found in *The Question of
Henry James*, edited by F. W. Dupee (New York: Henry Holt & Company,
Inc., 1945), and Philip Rahv's *Image and Idea* (New York: New Directions,
1949).

If the shadows of the physically dispossessed — the sweat and the bone-weariness and the manifold anonymous deprivation in which this culture-buying power had its source — are excluded from James's money-gilded canvas, the shadow of spiritual dispossession is the somber shape under the money outline. We are not allowed to forget the aesthetic and moral impoverishment that spread its gross vacuum at the core of the American acquisitive dream — the greed, the obtuse or rapacious presumption, the disvaluation of values that kept pace to pace with material expansion. James's characteristic thematic contrasts, here as in other novels, are those of surface against depth, inspection against experience, buying power against living power, the American tourist's cultural balcony against the European abyss of history and memory and involved motive where he perilously or callously teeters. In *The Portrait*, the American heroine's pilgrimage in Europe becomes a fatally serious spiritual investment, an investment of the "free" self in and with the circumstantial and binding past, a discovery of the relations of the self with history, and a moral renovation of history in the freedom of the individual conscience. It is a growing of more delicate and deeper-reaching roots and a nourishment of a more complex, more troubled, more creative personal humanity. It is, in short, what is ideally meant by "civilization," as that word refers to a process that can take place in an individual.

The postulate of wealth and privilege is, in revised terms, that of the second chapter of Genesis (the story of Adam in the garden) — that of the optimum conditions which will leave the innocent soul at liberty to develop its potentialities — and, as in the archetype of the Fall of Man, the postulate is significant not as excluding knowledge of good and evil, but as presenting a rare opportunity for such knowledge. It is the bounty poured on Isabel Archer (significantly, the man who gives her the symbolical investiture of money is a man who is fatally ill; significantly, also, she is under an illusion as to the giver) that makes her "free" to determine her choice of action, and thus morally most responsible for her choice; but it is the very bounty of her fortune, also, that activates at once, as if chemically, the proclivity to evil in the world of privilege that her wealth allows her to enter — it is her money that draws Madame Merle and Osmond to her; so that her "freedom" is actualized as imprisonment, in a peculiarly ashen and claustral, because peculiarly refined, suburb of hell. Isabel's quest had, at the earliest, been a quest for happiness — the naïvely egoistic American quest; it converts into a problem of spiritual salvation,

that is, into a quest of "life"; and again the Biblical archetype
shadows for the problem. After eating of the fruit of the tree of
knowledge of good and evil, how is one to regain access to the
tree of life?

The great fairy tales and saints' legends have identified life with
knowledge. For the fairy-tale hero, the fruit of the tree of life that
is the guerdon of kingdom is the golden fleece or the golden apples
that his wicked stepmother or usurping uncle have sent him in
quest of; and to achieve the guerdon he must go through all
tormenting knowledge — of serpents, floods, fire, ogres, enchant-
ment, and even of his own lusts and murderous capacities. The
ordeal of the heroes of saints' legends is also an ordeal of knowledge
of evil, and the guerdon is life. As do these ancient tales, *The
Portrait* identifies life with the most probing, dangerous, responsible
awareness — identifies, as it were, the two "trees," the tree of the
Fall and the tree of the Resurrection. The heroine's voluntary
search for fuller consciousness leads her, in an illusion of perfect
freedom to choose only "the best" in experience, to choose an evil;
but it is this that, by providing insight through suffering and guilt,
provides also access to life — to the fructification of consciousness
that is a knowledge of human bondedness. At the very end of the
book, Caspar Goodwood gives passionate voice to the illusion of
special privileges of choice and of a good to be had by exclusion
and separateness: he says to Isabel,

> "It would be an insult to you to assume that you care for . . . the
> bottomless idiocy of the world. We've nothing to do with all that;
> we're quite out of it . . . We can do absolutely as we please; to whom
> under the sun do we owe anything? What is it that holds us, what
> is it that has the smallest right to interfere . . . ? The world's all
> before us — and the world's very big."

Isabel answers at random. "The world's very small." What attitude
of mind takes her back to Rome, back to old evil and old servitude,
is not described; we know only that she does go back. But it is
evident that she does so because the "small" necessitous world
has received an extension, not in the horizontal direction of imperial
mobility that Gaspar Goodwood suggests, but an invisible extension
in depth, within her own mind — an extension in the freedom of
personal renunciation and inexhaustible responsibility. The knowledge she has acquired has been tragic knowledge, but her story
does not stop here, as it would if it were a tragedy — it goes on
out of the pages of the book, to Rome, where we cannot follow it;

for the knowledge has been the means to "life," and having learned to live, she must "live long," as she says. It is only the process of the learning that the portrait frame itself holds.

The title, *The Portrait*, asks the eye to see. And the handling of the book is in terms of seeing. The informing and strengthening of the eye of the mind is the theme — the ultimate knowledge, the thing finally "seen," having only the contingent importance of stimulating a more subtle and various activity of perception. The dramatization is deliberately "scenic," moving in a series of recognition scenes that are slight and low-keyed at first, or blurred and erroneous, in proportion both to the innocence of the heroine and others' skill in refined disguises and obliquities; then, toward the end, proceeding in swift and livid flashes. For in adopting as his compositional center the growth of a consciousness, James was able to use the bafflements and illusions of ignorance for his "complications," as he was able to use, more consistently than any other novelist, "recognitions" for his crises. Further, this action, moving through errors and illuminations of the inward eye, is set in a symbolic construct of things to be seen by the physical eye — paintings and sculptures, old coins and porcelain and lace and tapestries, most of all buildings: the aesthetic riches of Europe, pregnant with memory, with "histories within histories" of skills and motivations, temptations and suffering. The context of particulars offered to physical sight (and these may be settings, like English country houses or Roman ruins, or objects in the setting, like a porcelain cup or a piece of old lace draped on a mantel, or a person's face or a group of people — and the emphasis on the visual is most constant and notable not in these particulars, extensive as they are, but in the figurative language of the book, in metaphors using visual images as their vehicle) intensifies the meaning of "recognition" in those scenes where *sight* is *insight*, and provides a concrete embodiment of the ambiguities of "seeing."

In James's handling of the richly qualitative setting, it is characteristically significant that he suggests visual or scenic traits almost always in such a way that the emphasis is on *modulations of perception in the observer*. The "look" of things is a response of consciousness and varies with the observer; the "look" of things has thus the double duty of representing external stimuli, by indirection in their passage through consciousness, and of representing the observer himself. For instance, when Ralph takes Isabel through the picture gallery in the Touchett home, the "imperfect" but "genial" light of the bracketed lamps shows the pictures as "vague squares of rich colour," and the look of the pictures is Isabel's state at the moment — her eager and innately gifted sensibility and her almost complete ignorance, her conscious orientation toward an unknown "rich" mode of being that is beautiful but indeterminate. Let us take another example from late in the book. Directly after that conversation with Madame Merle when Isabel learns, with the full force of evil revelation, Madame Merle's part in her marriage, she goes out for a drive alone.

> She had long before this taken old Rome into her confidence, for in a world of ruins the ruin of her happiness seemed a less unnatural catastrophe. She rested her weariness upon things that had crumbled for centuries and yet still were upright; she dropped her secret sadness into the silence of lonely places, where its very modern quality detached itself and grew objective, so that as she sat in a sun-warmed angle on a winter's day, or stood in a mouldy church to which no one came, she could almost smile at it and think of its smallness. Small it was, in the large Roman record, and her haunting sense of the continuity of the human lot easily carried her from the less to the greater. She had become deeply, tenderly acquainted with Rome: it interfused and moderated her passion. But she had grown to think of it chiefly as the place where people had suffered. This was what came to her in the starved churches, where the marble columns, transferred from pagan ruins, seemed to offer her a companionship in endurance and the musty incense to be a compound of long-unanswered prayers.

Here the definition of visible setting — churches and marble columns and ruins, and comprehending all these, Rome — though it is full, is vague and diffuse, in the external sense of the "seen"; but in the sense that it is a setting evoked by Isabel's own deepened consciousness, it is exactly and clearly focused. It is Rome *felt*, felt as an immensity of human time, as a great human continuum of sadness and loneliness and passion and aspiration and patience; and it has this definition by virture of Isabel's personal ordeal and her perception of its meaning. The "vague squares of rich colour" have become determinate.

The theme of "seeing" (the theme of the developing consciousness) is fertile with ironies and ambiguities that arise from the natural symbolism of the act of seeing, upon which so vastly many of human responses and decisions are dependent. The eye, as it registers surfaces, is an organ of aesthetic experience, in the etymological sense of the word "aesthetic," which is a word deriving from a Greek verb meaning "to perceive" — to perceive through the senses. James provides his world with innumerable fine surfaces for this kind of perception; it is a world endowed with the finest selective opportunities for the act of "seeing," for aesthetic cultivation. But our biological dependence upon the eye has made it a symbol of intellectual and moral and spiritual perception, forms of perception which are — by the makers of dictionaries — discriminated radically from aesthetic perception. Much of James's work is an exploration of the profound identity of the aesthetic and the moral. (In this he is at variance with the makers of dictionaries, but he has the companionship of Socrates' teacher Diotima, as her teaching is represented by Plato in the *Symposium*. Diotima taught that the way to spiritual good lay through the hierarchies of the "beautiful," that is, through graduations from one form of aesthetic experience to another.) Aesthetic experience proper, since it is acquired through the senses, is an experience of *feeling*. But so also moral experience, when it is not sheerly nominal and ritualistic, is an experience of *feeling*. Neither one has reality — has psychological depth — unless it is "felt" (hence James's so frequent use of phrases such as "felt life" and "the very *taste* of life," phrases that insist on the feeling-base of complete and integrated living). Furthermore, both aesthetic and moral experience are nonutilitarian. The first distinction that aestheticians usually make, in defining the aesthetic, is its distinction from the useful; when the aesthetic is converted to utility, it becomes something else, its value designation is different — as when a beautiful bowl becomes valuable not for its beauty but for its capacity to hold soup. So also the moral, when it is converted to utility, becomes something else than the moral — becomes even immoral, a parody of or a blasphemy against the moral life (in our richest cultural heritage, both Hellenic and Christian, the moral life is symbolically associated with utter loss of utility goods and even with loss of physical life — as in the Gospel passage, "Leave all that thou hast and follow me," or as in the career of Socrates, or as in Sophocles' *Antigone*). Moral and aesthetic experience have then in common their foundation in feeling and their distinction from the useful. The identity that James explores is their identity in the most capacious and most integrated — the most "civilized" — consciousness, whose sense relationships (aesthetic relationships) with the external world of scenes and objects have the same quality and the same spiritual determination as its relationships with people (moral relationships). But his exploration of that ideal identity involves cognizance of failed integration, cognizance of the many varieties of one-sidedness

or one-eyedness or blindness that go by the name of the moral or
the aesthetic, and of the destructive potentialities of the human
consciousness when it is one-sided either way. His ironies revolve
on the ideal concept of a spacious integrity of feeling: feeling,
ideally, is *one* — and there is ironic situation when feeling is split
into the "moral" and the "aesthetic," each denying the other and
each posing as *all*.

There is comic irony in Henrietta Stackpole's moral busybodyness
as she flutters and sputters through Europe obtaining feature
materials for her home-town newspaper, "featuring" largely the
morally culpable un-Americanism of Europeans to serve her readers
as a flattering warning against indulgence in the aesthetic. Henrietta
is a stock James comedy character, and she is essential. Without
Henrietta's relative incapacity to "see" more than literal surfaces,
the significant contrast between surface and depth, between outward and inward "seeing," between undeveloped and developed
consciousness, would lose a needed demonstration. (But let us say
for Henrietta that, like Horatio in *Hamlet*, she is employed by
the dramatist for as many sorts of purposes as his scenes happen
to demand; when a foil of obtuseness is wanted, Henrietta is there,
and when a foil of good interpretive intelligence or plain charitable
generosity is wanted, Henrietta is also there. She is the type of
what James technically called the *ficelle*, a wholly subordinate
character immensely useful to take in confidences from the prin-
cipals and to serve other functions of "relief" — "relief" in that
sense in which the lower level of a relievo provides perspective for
the carved projections.) In Mrs. Touchett, what appears at first
as the comic irony of absolute aesthetic insensitivity accompanied
by a rugged moral dogmatism ("she had a little moral account-book
— with columns unerringly ruled and a sharp steel clasp — which
she kept with exemplary neatness") becomes at the end of the
book, with her son's death, the tragic irony of that kind of
ambiguous misery which is an inability to acknowledge or realize
one's own suffering, when suffering is real but the channels of
feeling have become nearly atrophied by lack of use. At the midday
meal, when Isabel and Mrs. Touchett come together after the night
of Ralph's death,

> Isabel saw her aunt not to be so dry as she appeared, and her old
> pity for the poor woman's inexpressiveness, her want of regret, of
> disappointment, came back to her. Unmistakably she would have

found it a blessing to-day to be able to feel a defeat, a mistake, even a shame or two. [Isabel] wondered if [her aunt] were not even missing those enrichments of consciousness and privately trying — reaching out for some aftertaste of life, dregs of the banquet: the testimony of pain or the old recreation of remorse. On the other hand perhaps she was afraid; if she should begin to know remorse at all it might take her too far. Isabel could perceive, however, how it had come over her dimly that she had failed of something, that she saw herself in the future as an old woman without memories. Her little sharp face looked tragical.

Mrs. Touchett's habitual moralistic denial of feeling as an aesthetic indulgence has left her deserted even by herself, even by her love of her son, even by memory, even by suffering. She is stranded in a morality that is tragically without meaning.

In Madame Merle and Osmond the ironies intrinsic to James's theme receive another turn. Madame Merle first appeals to Isabel's admiration by her capacity for "feeling" — for that kind of feeling to which the term "aesthetic" has been specially adapted in common modern use: feeling for the arts, the sensuous perceptivity underlying the arts, and, by extension, feeling for the finer conventions of manners as "arts of living." (Madame Merle "knew how to feel . . . This was indeed Madame Merle's great talent, her most perfect gift.") At Gardencourt, when she is not engaged in writing letters, she paints (she "made no more of brushing in a sketch than of pulling off her gloves") or she plays the piano (she "was a brave musician") or she is "employed upon wonderful tasks of rich embroidery." (The presentation is just a bit insidious, not only because of Madame Merle's so very great plasticity in going from one art to another, but also in the style of the phrases: the suggestion of conventional fluidity in the comparison of her ease in painting with the ease of "pulling off her gloves," the word "brave" — an honorific word in certain places, but carrying here the faintest note of bravado — and the word "employed," suggesting, as it reverberates, Madame Merle's not disinterested professional aestheticism.) Her senses are active and acute: walking in the English rain, she says,

"It never wets you and it always smells good." She declared that in England the pleasures of smell were great . . . and she used to lift the sleeve of her British overcoat and bury her nose in it, inhaling the clear, fine scent of the wool.

Just how acute her perceptions are is shown never more clearly than in that scene in which she learns of the distribution of property after Mr. Touchett's death, occurring in Chapter 20 of Volume I. Mrs. Touchett has just told her that Ralph, because of the state of his health, had hurried away from England before the reading of the will, in which Isabel had been left half of the fortune accruing to him. With this news, Madame Merle "remained thoughtful a moment, her eyes bent on the floor," and when Isabel enters the room, Madame Merle kisses her — this being "the only allusion the visitor, in her great good taste, made . . . to her young friend's inheritance." There are no other signs than these (and the episode is typical of James's minor "recognition scenes") of just how quickly and acutely Madame Merle's senses — her perception, her intuition — have functioned in apprising her of the possibilities of exploitation now opened, and in apprising her also of the fact that Ralph is the real donor of Isabel's fortune, a fact of which Isabel herself remains ignorant until Madame Merle viciously informs her. Madame Merle's feeling for situation is so subtly educated that she needs but the slightest of tokens in order to respond. And yet, with a sensitivity educated so exquisitely and working at such high tension she is morally insensible — or almost so; not quite — for, unlike Osmond, whose damnation is in ice where the moral faculty is quite frozen, she still has the spiritual capacity of those whose damnation is in fire, the capacity to know that she is damned.

Madame Merle and Osmond use their cultivated aestheticism for utility purposes — Madame Merle, to further her ambition for place and power; Osmond, to make himself separate and envied. Their debasement of the meaning of the aesthetic becomes symbolically vicious when it shows itself in their relationships with people — with Isabel, for instance, who is for them an object of virtu that differs from other objects of virtu in that it bestows money rather than costs it. This is the evil referred to by Kant in his second Categorical Imperative: the use of persons as means — an evil to which perhaps all evil in human relationships reduces. In the case of Madame Merle and Osmond, it has a peculiar and blasphemous ugliness, inasmuch as the atmosphere of beauty in which they live — beauty of surroundings and of manners — represents the finest, freest product of civilization and is such, ideally, as to induce the most reverential feeling for people as well as for things. Isabel first appeals to Osmond as being "as smooth to his general need of her as handled ivory to the palm": it is an "aesthetic" image suggesting his fastidiousness but, ironically, suggesting at the same time his coarseness — for while ivory, like pearls, may be the more beautiful for handling, "handled ivory" might also be the head of a walking stick, and it is in some sort as a walking stick that he uses Isabel. An extension of the same figure, without the aesthetic and with only the utilitarian connotation, indicates Osmond's real degeneracy: Isabel finally realizes that she has been for him "an applied handled hung-up tool, as senseless and convenient as mere wood and iron." But the evil is not one that can be isolated or confined; it is automatically proliferative. Morally dead himself, incapable of reverence for the human quality in others, Osmond necessarily tries to duplicate his death in them, for it is by killing their volition that he can make them useful; dead, they are alone "beautiful." He urges upon Isabel the obscene suggestion that she, in turn, "use" Lord Warburton by exploiting Warburton's old love for herself in order to get him to marry Pansy; and Osmond can find no excuse for her refusal except that she has her private designs for "using" the Englishman. But it is in Osmond's use of Pansy, his daughter, that he is most subtly and horribly effective. He has made her into a work of art, the modeling materials being the least artful of childish qualities — her innocence and gentleness; and he has almost succeeded in reducing her will to an echo of his own. The quaint figure of Pansy, always only on the edge of scenes, is of great structural importance in the latter half of the book; for she shows the full measure of the abuse that Isabel resists, and it is to nourish in her whatever small germ of creative volition may remain — to salvage, really, a life — that Isabel returns to Rome and to Osmond's paralyzing ambiance.

The moral question that is raised by every character in the book is a question of the "amount of felt life" that each is able to experience, a question of how many and how various are the relationships each can, with integrity, enter into. Or, to put the matter in its basic metaphor, it is a question of how much each person is able to "see," and not only to see but to compose into creative order. The moral question, since it involves vision, feeling, and composition, is an aesthetic one as well. Madame Merle and Osmond are blind to certain relations: "I don't pretend to know what people are meant for," Madame Merle says, ". . . I only know what I can do with them." Mrs. Touchett is blind to certain others. Let us stop for a moment with Henrietta Stackpole's comic crudity of vision, for the "eye" is all-important, and the ranges of vision really begin with an eye like that of Henrietta. It is "a peculiarly open, surprised-looking eye." "The most striking point in her appearance was the remarkable fixedness of this organ."

> She fixed her eyes on [Ralph], and there was something in their character that reminded him of large polished buttons — buttons that might have fixed the elastic loops of some tense receptacle: he seemed to see the reflection of surrounding objects on the pupil. The expression of a button is not usually deemed human, but there was something in Miss Stackpole's gaze that made him, a very modest man, feel vaguely embarrassed — less inviolate, more dishonoured, than he liked.

Henrietta, with her gregariously refractive button-sight, has also "clear-cut views on most subjects . . . she knew perfectly in advance what her opinions would be." Henrietta's is the made-up consciousness, the pseudo consciousness, that is not a process but a content hopelessly once and for all given, able to refract light but not to take it in. (We can understand Henrietta's importance, caricatural as she is, by the fact that she is the primitive form of the pseudo consciousness which Madame Merle and Osmond, in their so much more sophisticated ways, exhibit: theirs too is the made-up consciousness, a rigidified content, impervious and uncreative.) The Misses Molyneux, Lord Warburton's sisters, have "eyes like the balanced basins, the circles of 'ornamental water,' set, in parterres, among the geraniums." Let us note that the figure is drawn from an "aesthetic" arrangement, that of formal gardens — and in this sense has directly opposite associations to those of Henrietta's buttons (presumably very American, very *useful* buttons). The Misses Molyneux's eyes, like Henrietta's, also merely reflect surrounding objects, and reflect more limitedly, far less mobily; but the image is significant of certain kinds of feeling, of "seeing," that Henrietta is incapable of, and that have derived from ancient disciplines in human relationships — contemplative feeling, reverence, feeling for privacy and for grace. Extremely minor figures such as these, of the buttons and the basins, are pregnant with the extraordinarily rich, extraordinarily subtle potentialities of the theme of "seeing" as an infinitely graduated cognizance of relations between self and world.

    In this book, the great range of structural significance through figurative language is due to the fact that whatever image vehicle a figure may have — even when the image is not itself a visual one — the general context is so deeply and consistently characterized by acts of "seeing" that every metaphor has this other implied extension of meaning. For example, a very intricate and extensive symbolic construct is built on a metaphor of opening doors. Henrietta, Ralph says, "walks in without knocking at the door." "She's too personal," he adds. As her eyes indiscriminately take in everything that is literally to be seen, so she walks in without knocking at the door of personality: "she thinks one's door should stand ajar." The correspondence of eyes and doors lies in the publicity Henrietta assumes (she is a journalist): her eye is public like a button, and responds as if everything else were public, as if there were no doors, as if there were nothing to be seen but what the public (the American newspaper public) might see without effort and without discomfort. In James's thematic system of surfaces and depths, "sight" is something achieved and not given, achieved in the loneliness of the individual soul and in the lucidity of darkness suffered; privacy is its necessary stamp, and it cannot be loaned or broadcast any more than can the loneliness or the suffering. "I keep a band of music in my ante-room," Ralph tells Isabel.

"It has orders to play without stopping; it renders me two excellent services. It keeps the sounds of the world from reaching the private apartments, and it makes the world think that dancing's going on within."

The notation has its pathos through Ralph's illness. Isabel "would have liked to pass through the ante-room . . . and enter the private apartments." It is only at the end, through her own revelations of remorse and loss, that those doors open to her.

The ironic force of the metaphor of doors, as it combines with the metaphor of "seeing," has a different direction in the crucial scene in Chapter 51 of the second volume — one of the major "recognition scenes" in the book, where Isabel sees Osmond's full malignancy, a malignancy the more blighting as it takes, and sincerely takes, the form of honor, and where Osmond sees unequivocally the vivid, mysterious resistance of a life that he has not been able to convert into a tool. Isabel comes to tell him that Ralph is dying and that she must go to England. She opens the door of her husband's study without knocking.

"Excuse me for disturbing you," she said.
"When I come to your room I always knock," he answered, going on with his work.
"I forgot; I had something else to think of. My cousin's dying."

"Ah, I don't believe that," said Osmond, looking at his drawing
through a magnifying glass. "He was dying when we married; he'll
outlive us all."

Osmond is here engaged in an activity representative of a man of
taste and a "collector" — he is making traced copies of ancient
coins (the fact that it is an act of tracing, of copying, has its own
significance, as has the object of his attention: coins). What he
"sees" in the situation that Isabel describes to him is quite exactly
what he sees in the fact that she has opened the door without
knocking: a transgression of convention; and what he does not
see is the right of another human being to feel, to love, to will
individually. Further, what he appallingly does not see is his
dependence, for the fortune Isabel has brought him, on the selfless
imagination of the dying man, Ralph; or, even more appallingly
(for one can scarcely suppose that Madame Merle had left him
ignorant of the source of Isabel's weath), what he does not see
is any reason for the moral responsibility implied by "gratitude,"
a defect of vision that gives a special and hideous bleakness to his
use of the word "grateful," when he tells Isabel that she has not
been "grateful" for his tolerance of her esteem for Ralph. The
metaphor of the "doors" thus goes through its changes, each
associated with a depth or shallowness, a straightness or obliquity
of vision, from Henrietta's aggressive myopia, to Ralph's reticence
and insight, to Osmond's refined conventionalism and moral
astigmatism.

Let us consider in certain other examples this reciprocity between theme and metaphor, insight and sight, image and eye.
Isabel's native choice is creativity, a "free exploration of life,"
but exploration is conducted constantly — vision is amplified constantly — at the cost of renunciations. It is in the "grey depths"
of the eyes of the elder Miss Molyneux, those eyes like the balanced basins of water set in parterres, that Isabel recognizes what
she has had to reject in rejecting Lord Warburton: "the peace,
the kindness, the honour, the possessions, a deep security and a
great exclusion." Caspar Goodwood has eyes that "seemed to
shine through the vizard of a helmet." He appears always as an
armor-man: "she saw the different fitted parts of him as she had
seen, in museums and portraits, the different fitted parts of armoured warriors — in plates of steel handsomely inlaid with gold."
"He might have ridden, on a plunging steed, the whirlwind of a
great war." The image is one of virility, but of passion without

relation, aggressive energy without responsibility. The exclusions implied by Caspar's steel-plated embrace are as great as those implied by the honor and the peace that Lord Warburton offers; and yet Isabel's final refusal of Caspar and of sexual possession is tragic, for it is to a sterile marriage that she returns.

Architectural images, and metaphors whose vehicle (like doors and windows) is associated with architecture, subtend the most various and complex of the book's meanings; and the reason for their particular richness of significance seems to be that, of all forms that are offered to sight and interpretation, buildings are the most natural symbols of civilized life, the most diverse also as to what their fronts and interiors can imply of man's relations with himself and with the outer world. Osmond's house in Florence has an "imposing front" of a "somewhat incommunicative character."

> It was the mask, not the face of the house. It had heavy lids, but no eyes; the house in reality looked another way — looked off behind . . . The windows of the ground-floor, as you saw them from the piazza, were, in their noble proportions, extremely architectural; but their function seemed less to offer communication with the world than to defy the world to look in . . .

(One notes again here the characteristic insistence on *eyes* and *looking.*) The description, perfectly fitting an old and noble Florentine villa, exactly equates with Osmond himself, and not only Isabel's first illusional impression of him — when it is his renunciatory reserve that attracts her, an appearance suggesting those "deeper rhythms of life" that she seeks — but also her later painful knowledge of the face behind the mask, which, like the house, is affected with an obliquity of vision, "looked another way — looked off behind." The interior is full of artful images; the group of people gathered there "might have been described by a painter as composing well"; even the footboy "might, tarnished as to livery and quaint as to type, have issued from some stray sketch of old-time manners, been 'put in' by the brush of a Longhi or a Goya"; the face of little Pansy is "painted" with a "fixed and intensely sweet smile." Osmond's world, contained within his eyeless house, is "sorted, sifted, arranged" for the eye; even his daughter is one of his arrangements. It is a world bred of ancient disciplines modulating through time, selection and composition, to the purest aesthetic form.

> [Isabel] carried away an image from her visit to his hill-top . . . which put on for her a particular harmony with other supposed and

divined things, histories within histories . . . It spoke of the kind of
personal issue that touched her most nearly; of the choice between
objects, subjects, contacts — what might she call them? — of a thin
and those of a rich association . . . of a care for beauty and perfection
so natural and so cultivated together that the career appeared to
stretch beneath it in the disposed vistas and with the ranges of steps
and terraces and fountains of a formal Italian garden.

The illusion is one of a depth and spaciousness and delicacy of
relationships, an illusion of the civilized consciousness.

But while Osmond's world suggests depth, it is, ironically, a
world of surfaces only, for Osmond has merely borrowed it. The
architectural metaphor shifts significantly in the passage (Chapter
42 of Volume II) in which Isabel takes the full measure of her
dwelling. "It was the house of darkness, the house of dumbness,
the house of suffocation."

> She had taken all the first steps in the purest confidence, and then
> she had suddenly found the infinite vista of a multiplied life to be a
> dark, narrow alley with a dead wall at the end. Instead of leading
> to the high places of happiness . . . it led rather downward and
> earthward, into realms of restriction and depression where the sound
> of other lives, easier and freer, was heard from above. . . .

"When she saw this rigid system close about her, draped though
it was in pictured tapestries . . . she seemed shut up with an odour
of mould and decay." Again the architectural image changes its
shape in that passage (quoted earlier in this essay) where Isabel
takes her knowledge and her sorrow into Rome, a Rome of architectural ruins. Here also are depth of human time, "histories within
histories," aesthetic form, but not "arranged," not borrowable,
not to be "collected" — only to be *lived* in the creative recognitions
brought to them by a soul itself alive. The image that accompanies
Ralph through the book — "his serenity was but the array of wild
flowers niched in his ruin" — gains meaning from the architectural
images so frequent in the Roman scenes (as, for instance, from
this:

> [Isabel] had often ascended to those desolate ledges from which the
> Roman crowd used to bellow applause and where now the wild
> flowers . . . bloom in the deep crevices . . .)

Whereas Osmond's forced "arrangements" of history and art and
people are without racination, blighting and lifeless, Ralph's "array

of wild flowers" is rooted, even if precariously rooted in a ruin; it is a life *grown*, grown in history, fertilized in the crevices of a difficult experience. The metaphor is another version of St. John's "Except a corn of wheat fall into the ground and die, it abideth alone; but if it die, it bringeth forth much fruit." Isabel, still seeking that freedom which is growth, goes back to Osmond's claustral house, for it is there, in the ruin where Pansy has been left, that she has placed roots, found a crevice in which to grow straightly and freshly, found a fertilizing, civilizing relationship between consciousness and circumstances.

Arnold Kettle

Henry James: *The Portrait of a Lady*

Compared with this the English novels which precede it, except perhaps those of Jane Austen, all seem a trifle crude. There is a habit of perfection here, a certainty and a poise, which is quite different from the merits and power of *Oliver Twist* or *Wuthering Heights* or even *Middelmarch*. The quality has something to do with the full consciousness of Henry James's art. Nothing in *The Portrait of a Lady* is unconscious, nothing there by chance, no ungathered wayward strands, no clumsiness. No novelist is so absorbed as James in what he himself might call his 'game.' But it is not an empty or superficial concern with 'form' that gives *The Portrait of a Lady* its quality. James's manner, his obsession with style, his intricate and passionate concern with presentation, do not spring from a narrow 'aesthetic' attitude to his art.

"James had in his style and perhaps in the life which it reflected an idiosyncrasy so powerful, so overweening, that to many it seemed a stultifying vice, or at least an inexcusable heresy. . . . He enjoyed an excess of intelligence and he suffered, both in life and art, from an excessive effort to communicate it, to represent it in all its full-

From *An Introduction to the English Novel,* II (London: Hutchinson Publishing Group, Ltd., 1953), 13-34. Reprinted by permission of the publisher.

ness. His style grew elaborate in the degree that he rendered shades and refinements of meaning and feeling not usually rendered at all. . . . His intention and all his labour was to represent dramatically intelligence at its most difficut, its most lucid, its most beautiful point. This is the sum of his idiosyncrasy."[1]

The Portrait of a Lady is not one of James's 'difficult' novels; but Mr. Blackmur's remarks usefully remind us of the inadequacy of a merely formal approach to James's work. The extraordinary richness of texture of his novels makes such an approach tempting; but it will take us neither to James's triumphs nor to his failures.

The beauty of texture derives immediately from two qualities, which are ultimately inseparable. One is James's ability to make us know his characters more richly, though not necessarily more vividly, than we know the characters of other novelists; the other is the subtlety of his own standpoint. Without the latter quality the former would not, of course, be possible. You cannot control the responses of your reader unless you are in complete control of your material.

In *The Portrait of a Lady* there are — looking at the question from an analytical point of view — two kinds of characters: those whom we know from straightforward, though not unsubtle, description by the author and those who reveal themselves in the course of the book. The latter are, obviously, the important ones. The former—Mrs. Touchett, Henrietta Stackpole, the Countess Gemini, Pansy Osmond — are interesting primarily in their relationship to the chief characters, in their part in the pattern; we do not follow their existence out of their function in the book. But they are nevertheless not 'flat' characters. They come alive not as 'characters,' not as personified 'humours,' but as complete people (Pansy, perhaps, is the exception, but then is not the intention that we should see her as scarcely an independent being at all?) and if we do not follow them out of the part of the plot which concerns them it is because our interests are more involved elsewhere, not because they do not have a full existence of their own.

The way Henry James introduces his characters to us depends entirely on the kind of function they are to have in his story. The main characters are never described as they *are* (i.e. as the author knows them to be) but — by and large — as Isabel Archer sees them. We know them at first only by the first impression that they make. We get to know better what they are like in the way

---

[1] R. P. Blackmur: Introduction to H. James, *The Art of the Novel* (1934), p. xii.

that, in life, we get to know people better through acquaintance. And just as in life we are seldom, if ever, quite certain what another person is like, so in a Henry James novel we are often pretty much at sea about particular characters for considerable portions of the book. In *The Portrait of a Lady* the person whom at first we inevitably know least about is Madame Merle. Henry James lets us know right from the start that there is something sinister about her; we are made quickly to feel that Isabel's reaction to her is less than adequate, but the precise nature of her character is not revealed until fairly far into the book.

It is not quite true to say that everything in *The Portrait of a Lady* is revealed through Isabel's consciousness. We know, from the start, certain things that Isabel does not know. We know, for instance — and twice Henry James explicitly reminds us of it — more about Ralph Touchett's feeling for Isabel than she herself perceives.

Indeed, there is a sense in which the novel is revealed to us through Ralph's consciousness, for his is the 'finest,' the fullest intelligence in the book and therefore he sees things — about Madame Merle, about Osmond, about Isabel herself — which Isabel does not see and inevitably such perceptions are transmitted to the reader. Again, we are offered important scenes — between Madame Merle and Osmond, between the Countess and Madame Merle — which reveal to us not the whole truth but enough of the truth about Madame Merle's stratagems to put us at an advantage over Isabel.

The truth is that Henry James's purpose in this novel is not to put Isabel between the reader and the situation (in the way that Strether's consciousness is used in *The Ambassadors*) but to reveal to the reader the full implications of Isabel's consciousness. For this to happen we must see Isabel not merely from the inside (i.e. know how she feels) but from the outside too. The method is, in fact, precisely the method of *Emma*, except that Jane Austen is rather more scrupulously consistent than Henry James. The scenes 'outside' Emma herself (like Jane Fairfax's visits to the post office) are brought to our knowledge by being related by a third party in the presence of Emma herself. Our only 'advantage' over Emma herself is provided by the words which Jane Austen uses to describe her. Henry James, as we have seen, takes greater liberties. Yet it is worth observing that the great scene at the centre of *The Portrait of a Lady* (Chapter XLII), in which

Isabel takes stock of her situation, is of precisely the same *kind* as the scene in which (Vol. I, Chapter XVI) Emma takes stock of her dealings with Harriet.

Since James's purpose is to render the full implications of Isabel's situation it is necessary that we should know more than Isabel, should see her, that is to say, from the outside. The question remains: how *much* more should we know? And James's answer is: just as much as is necessary for a fully sympathetic understanding. Thus we are to know that Madame Merle has drawn Isabel into a trap, but we are not to know why. The full story is kept back, not because Henry James is interested in suspense in the melodramatic sense, but because if we were in on the secret the nature of Isabel's discovery of her situation could not be so effectively revealed. It is necessary to the novel that we should *share* Isabel's suspicions and her awakening. In order to give the precise weight (not just the logical weight but the intricate weight of feelings, standards, loyalties) to the issues involved in her final dilemma we must know not just what has happened to Isabel but the way it has happened.

It is from such a consideration that there will emerge one of Henry James's cardinal contributions to the art of the novel. With James the question "What happened?" carries the most subtle, the most exciting ramifications. To no previous novelist had the answer to such a question seemed so difficult, its implications so interminable. To a George Eliot the question is complicated enough: to understand what happened to Lydgate we must be made aware of innumerable issues, facets of character, moral choices, social pressures. And yet deep in George Eliot's novel is implicit the idea that if the reader only knows enough facts about the situation he will know the situation. It is the aim of Henry James to avoid the 'about' or, at least, to alter its status, to transform quantity into quality. His is the poet's ambition: to create an object about which we say not "It means. . . ." but "It is. . . ." (In this he is with Emily Brontë.) We cannot *understand* Isabel Archer, he implies, unless we feel as she feels. And it is, indeed, because he succeeds in this attempt that *The Portrait of a Lady* though not a greater novel than *Middlemarch* is a more moving one.

As a rule when Henry James describes a character (as opposed to allowing the person to be revealed in action) the description is of the kind we have noticed in *Emma* or *Middlemarch*.

"Mrs. Touchett was certainly a person of many oddities, of which her behaviour on returning to her husband's house after many months was a noticeable specimen. She had her own way of doing all that she did, and this is the simplest description of a character which, although by no means without liberal motions, rarely succeeded in giving an impression of suavity. Mrs. Touchett might do a great deal of good, but she never pleased. This way of her own, of which she was so fond, was not intrinsically offensive — it was just unmistakeably distinguished from the way of others. The edges of her conduct were so very clear-cut that for susceptible persons it sometimes had a knife-like effect. That hard fineness came out in her deportment during the first hours of her return from America, under circumstances in which it might have seemed that her first act would have been to exchange greetings with her husband and son. Mrs. Touchett, for reasons which she deemed excellent, always retired on such occasions into impenetrable seclusion, postponing the more sentimental ceremony until she had repaired the disorder of dress with a completeness which had the less reason to be of high importance as neither beauty nor vanity were concerned in it. She was a plain-faced old woman, without graces and without any great elegance, but with an extreme respect for her own motives. She was usually prepared to explain these — when the explanation was asked as a favour; and in such a case they proved totally different from those that had been attributed to her. She was virtually separated from her husband, but she appeared to perceive nothing irregular in the situation. It had become clear, at an early stage of their community, that they should never desire the same thing at the same moment, and this appearance had prompted her to rescue disagreement from the vulgar realm of accident. She did what she could to erect it into a law — a much more edifying aspect of it — by going to live in Florence, where she bought a house and established herself; and by leaving her husband to take care of the English branch of his bank. This arrangement greatly pleased her; it was so felicitously definite. It struck her husband in the same light, in a foggy square in London, where it was at times the most definite face he discerned; but he would have preferred that such unnatural things should have a greater vagueness. To agree to disagree had cost him an effort; he was ready to agree to almost anything but that, and saw no reason why either assent or dissent should be so terribly consistent.

Mrs. Touchett indulged in no regrets nor speculations, and usually came once a year to spend a month with her husband, a period during which she apparently took pains to convince him that she had adopted the right system. She was not fond of the English style of life, and had three or four reasons for it to which she currently alluded; they bore upon minor points of that ancient order, but for Mrs. Touchett they amply justified non-residence. She detested bread-sauce, which, as she said, looked like a poultice and tasted like soap; she objected to the consumption of beer by her maid-servants; and she affirmed that the British laundress (Mrs. Touchett was very particular about the appearance of her linen) was not a mistress of her art."[2]

Here the description depends for its effect entirely on the quality of the author's wit, his organized intellectual comment, and the wit is of the sort (a penetrating delicacy of observation within an accepted social group) achieved by Jane Austen or George Eliot.

But some of the described characters in *The Portrait of a Lady* come poetically to life. This is the description of Isabel's first meeting with the Countess Gemini.

"The Countess Gemini simply nodded without getting up; Isabel could see she was a woman of high fashion. She was thin and dark and not at all pretty, having features that suggested some tropical bird — a long beak-like nose, small, quickly-moving eyes and a mouth and chin that receded extremely. Her expression, however, thanks to various intensities of emphasis and wonder, of horror and joy, was not inhuman, and, as regards her appearance, it was plain she understood herself and made the most of her points. Her attire, voluminous and delicate, bristling with elegance, had the look of shimmering plumage, and her attitudes were as light and sudden as those of a creature who perched upon twigs. She had a great deal of manner; Isabel, who had never known anyone with so much manner, immediately classed her as the most affected of women. She remembered that Ralph had not recommended her as an acquaintance; but she was ready to acknowledge that to a casual view the Countless Gemini revealed no depths. Her demonstrations suggested the violent wavings of some flag of general truce — white silk with fluttering streamers."[3]

We are never to get to know the Countess very well, but already we see her with a peculiar vividness, the vividness evoked by poetic imagery. The bird image has a visual force so intense that it goes beyond surface illumination — "bristling with elegance" in its context contains a world of comment as well as vividness. So does the image of the flag of truce.

---

[2] *The Portrait of a Lady,* Chap. III.
[3] Ibid., Chap. XXIV.

Henry James's predominant interest is, however, by no means in character. *The Portrait of a Lady*, he tells us in his Preface, has as its corner-stone "the conception of a certain young woman affronting her destiny." The interest, it is already indicated, is not primarily a psychological one, not a matter of mere personal analysis. And *The Portrait of a Lady* is indeed a novel of the widest scope and relevance. Though it is in the line of Jane Austen it has a quality which it is not misleading to call symbolic (already we have hinted at a link with what would appear at first to be a wholly different novel, *Wuthering Heights*). *The Portrait of a Lady* is a novel about destiny. Or, to use a concept rather more in tone with the language of the book itself, it is a novel about freedom. It would not be outrageous, though it might be misleading, to call it a nineteenth-century *Paradise Lost*.

Henry James is, of course, far too sophisticated an artist to offer us the 'subject' of his book on a platter. In his moral interest he avoids like the plague anything approaching the abstract.

> "I might envy," he writes in his Preface, "though I couldn't emulate, the imaginative writer so constituted as to see his fable first and to make out its agents afterwards: I could think so little of any fable that didn't need its agents positively to launch it; I could think so little of any situation that didn't depend for its interest on the nature of the persons situated, and thereby on their way of taking it."

And again, a little later:

> "There is, I think, no more nutritive or suggestive truth in this connexion than that of the perfect dependence of the 'moral' sense of a work of art on the amount of felt life concerned in producing it."*

James's novel is not a moral fable; but its moral interest is nevertheless central. Only the business of "launching," of presenting with all the necessary depth of "felt life," that "ado" which is the story of Isabel Archer, all this may easily distract our attention from the central theme. Indeed there was a time when James's novels apparently were regarded as "comedies of manners"

---

*I quote with some uneasiness from James's Preface (written, it will be recalled, some quarter of a century after the novel), not because I doubt the relevance or interest of his observations but because I am conscious of the difficulty of assimilating out of context sentences written in his most idiosyncratic, complex style.

(cf. Trollope) and even so superbly intelligent a reader as E. M. Forster seems to have missed the point of them almost completely. The launching of *The Portrait of a Lady* is beautifully done. Gardencourt, the house in Albany, upper-class London: they are called up with magnificent certainty and solidity. So too are the people of the book: the Touchetts, Caspar Goodwood, Henrietta Stackpole, Lord Warburton, Isabel herself. If these characters are to contribute to a central pattern it will not be, it is clear, in the manner of anything approaching allegory. They are all too 'round,' too 'free' to be felt, for even a moment, simply to be 'standing for' anything. It is one of Henry James's achievements that he can convince us that his characters have a life outside the pages of his novel without ever leading us into the temptation of following them beyond his purpose. It is because everything in these early chapters of *The Portrait of a Lady* is realized with such fullness, such apparent lack of pointed emphasis, that we are slow to recognize the basic pattern of the novel, but it is also on this account that our imagination is so firmly engaged.

Before the end of the first chapter, however, a subsidiary theme has already been fairly fully stated and three of the main themes announced or, at any rate, indicated. The subsidiary theme is that generally referred to in Henry James's novels as the international situation — the relation of America to Europe. Graham Greene in a recent introduction to *The Portrait of a Lady* has tried to play down the importance of this theme. "It is true the innocent figure is nearly always American (Roderick Hudson, Newman, Isabel and Milly, Maggie Verver and her father), but the corrupted characters . . . are also American: Mme. Merle, Gilbert Osmond, Kate Croy, Merton Densher, Charlotte Stant. His characters are mainly American, simply because James himself was American."[4] In fact, of course, neither Kate Croy nor Densher is an American and one of the points about the other "corrupted" characters is that they are all expatriates, europeanized Americans, whom it is at least possible to see as corrupted by Europe.* The theme of the impact of European civilization on Americans — innocent or not — is not a main theme of *The Portrait of a Lady* but it is nevertheless there and we shall return to it later. And it is broached in the very first pages of the novel in the description of the Touchett *ménage* and in such details as the failure of Mr.

---

[4] Ibid., Introduction (World Classics, ed.), p. ix.
*For a fuller discussion of this problem see *Henry James, the Major Phase* by F. O. Matthiessen and *Maule's Curse* by Yvor Winters.

Touchett to understand (or rather, his pretence at not understanding) Lord Warburton's jokes.

The main themes indicated in the first chapters are the importance of wealth, the difficulty of marriage and — fundamental to the other two — the problem of freedom or independence. In each case the theme appears to be merely a casual subject of conversation but in fact there is nothing casual there. The vital theme of freedom is introduced in the form of a joke — one of Mrs. Touchett's eccentric telegrams: " 'Changed hotel, very bad, impudent clerk, address here. Taken sister's girl, died last year, go to Europe, two sisters, quite independent'." The telegram is discussed by Mr. Touchett and Ralph.

> " 'There's one thing very clear in it,' said the old man; 'she has given the hotel-clerk a dressing.'
> 'I'm not sure even of that, since he has driven her from the field. We thought at first that the sister mentioned might be the sister of the clerk; but the subsequent mention of a niece seems to prove that the allusion is to one of my aunts. Then there was a question as to whose the two other sisters were; they are probably two of my late aunt's daughters. But who's "quite independent," and in what sense is the term used? — that point's not yet settled. Does the expression apply more particularly to the young lady my mother has adopted, or does it characterize her sisters equally? — and is it used in a moral or in a financial sense? Does it mean that they've been left well off, or that they wish to be under no obligations? — or does it simply mean that they're fond of their own way?' "[5]

Ralph's frivolous speculations do in fact state the basic problems to be dealt with in the novel. The point is indeed not yet settled: it will take the whole book to settle it. And, even then, 'settle' is not the right word. One does not, Henry James would be quick to remind us, settle life.

The independence of Isabel is the quality about her most often emphasized. Mrs. Touchett has taken her up, but she is not, she assures Ralph "a candidate for adoption." " 'I'm very fond of my liberty',"[6] she adds. From the very first the ambiguous quality of this independence is stressed. Isabel is attractive, interesting, 'fine' ("she carried within her a great fund of life, and her deepest enjoyment was to feel the continuity between the movements of

---

[5] Ibid., Chap. I.
[6] Ibid., Chap. II.

her own soul and the agitations of the world"[7]); but she is also in many respects inexperienced, naïve. " 'It occurred to me,' Mrs. Touchett says, 'that it would be a kindness to take her about and introduce her to the world. She thinks she knows a great deal of it — like most American girls; but like most American girls she's ridiculously mistaken'."[8] Henry James does not allow us, charming creature as she is, to idealize Isabel:

"Altogether, with her meagre knowledge, her inflated ideals, her confidence at once innocent and dogmatic, her temper at once exacting and indulgent, her mixture of curiosity and fastidiousness, of vivacity and indifference, her desire to look very well and to be if possible even better, her determination to see, to try, to know, her combination of the delicate desultory flame-like spirit and the eager and personal creature of conditions: she would be an easy victim of scientific criticism: if she were not intended to awaken on the reader's part an impulse more tender and more purely expectant."[9]

The Portrait of a Lady is the revelation of the inadequacy of Isabel's view of freedom.

The revelation is so full, so concrete, that to abstract from it the main, insistent theme must inevitably weaken the impression of the book. But analysis involves such abstraction and we shall not respond fully to James's novel unless we are conscious of its theme. The theme in its earlier stages is fully expressed in the scene in which Caspar Goodwood for the second time asks Isabel to marry him (she has just refused Lord Warburton).

" 'I don't know,' she answered rather grandly. 'The world — with all these places so arranged and so touching each other — comes to strike one as rather small.'

'It's a sight too big for me!' Caspar exclaimed with a simplicity our young lady might have found touching if her face had not been set against concessions.

This attitude was part of a system, a theory, that she had lately embraced, and to be thorough she said after a moment: 'Don't think me unkind if I say it's just that — being out of your sight — that I like. If you were in the same place I should feel you were watching me, and I don't like that — I like my liberty too much. If there's a thing in the world I'm fond of,' she went on with a slight recurrence

[7]Ibid., Chap. IV.
[8]Ibid., Chap. V.
[9]Ibid., Chap. VI.

of grandeur, 'it's my personal independence.' But whatever there might be of the too superior in this speech moved Caspar Goodwood's admiration; there was nothing he winced at in the large air of it. He had never supposed she hadn't wings and the need of beautiful free movements — he wasn't, with his own long arms and strides, afraid of any force in her. Isabel's words, if they had been meant to shock him, failed of the mark and only made him smile with the sense that here was common ground. 'Who would wish less to curtail your liberty than I? What can give me greater pleasure than to see you perfectly independent — doing whatever you like? It's to make you independent that I want to marry you.'

'That's a beautiful sophism,' said the girl with a smile more beautiful still.

'An unmarried woman — a girl of your age — isn't independent. There are all sorts of things she can't do. She's hampered at every step.'

'That's as she looks at the question,' Isabel answered with much spirit. 'I'm not in my first youth — I can do what I choose — I belong quite to the independent class. I've neither father nor mother; I'm poor and of a serious disposition; I'm not pretty. I therefore am not bound to be timid and conventional; indeed I can't afford such luxuries. Besides, I try to judge things for myself; to judge wrong, I think, is more honourable than not to judge at all. I don't wish to be a mere sheep in the flock; I wish to choose my fate and know something of human affairs beyond what other people think it compatible with propriety to tell me.' She paused a moment, but not long enough for her companion to reply. He was apparently on the point of doing so when she went on: 'Let me say this to you, Mr. Goodwood. You're so kind as to speak of being afraid of my marrying. If you should hear a rumour that I'm on the point of doing so — girls are liable to have such things said about them — remember what I have told you about my love of liberty and venture to doubt it'."[10]

The Portrait of a Lady is far from allegory yet one is permitted to feel, in the symbolic quality of the novel, that the characters, though unmistakably individuals, are more than individuals. Thus, in her rejection of Caspar Goodwood, Isabel is rejecting America, or at least that part of America that Goodwood represents, young, strong, go-ahead, uninhibited, hard. For Goodwood (as for Henrietta, who essentially shares his quality) the problem of freedom is simple and might be expressed in the words of Mr. Archibald Macleish's American Dream:

---

[10]Ibid., Chap. XVI.

"America is promises
For those that take them."

Goodwood — and it would be wrong to see him as a wholly unsympathetic character — is prepared to take them with all that taking implies. To him and Henrietta (and they are, on one level, the most sensible, positive people in the book) Isabel's problem is not a problem at all. Freedom for them has the simple quality it possessed for the nineteenth-century liberal.

The rejection of Lord Warburton has, similarly, a symbolic quality — though, again, one must insist that this is not an allegory. Warburton is a liberal aristocrat. He embodies the aristocratic culture of Europe (that has so attracted Isabel at Gardencourt) and adds his own reforming ideas — a combination which Henry James, had he been the kind of aesthetic snob he is often held to be, might have found irresistible. Ralph Touchett sums up Warburton's social position magnificently:

" '. . . He says I don't understand my time, I understand it certainly better than he, who can neither abolish himself as a nuisance nor maintain himself as an institution'." [11]

Isabel's rejection of Lord Warburton is not a light one. She feels very deeply the attraction of the aristocratic standards. But she feels also the limitations of Warburton and his sisters, the Misses Molyneux (it is worth comparing them with another 'county' family — the Marchants — in the wonderful *Princess Casamassima;* Henry James's attitude to the British aristocracy is by no means uncritical).

" '. . . So long as I look at the Misses Molyneux they seem to me to answer a kind of ideal. Then Henrietta presents herself, and I'm straightway convinced by *her;* not so much in respect to herself as in respect to what masses behind her'." [12]

Ralph, too, (though he does not undervalue her) disposes of Henrietta:

" 'Henrietta . . . does smell of the Future — it almost knocks one down!' " [13]

---

[11] Ibid., Chap. VIII.
[12] Ibid., Chap. X.
[13] Ibid., Chap. X.

Goodwood and Warburton rejected (almost like two temptations), Isabel is now 'free' to affront her destiny. But she is not
free because she is poor. She has never, we are told early on, known
anything about money, and it is typical of this novel that this fine,
romantic indifference to wealth should be one of the basic factors
in Isabel's tragedy.

Henry James's characters always have to be rich and the reason
is not the obvious one. "I call people rich," says Ralph Touchett,
"when they're able to meet the requirements of their imagination."[14]
It is for this reason that he persuades his father to leave Isabel a
fortune. She must be rich in order to be free of the material world.
She must be free in order to 'live.'

It is Ralph's one supreme mistake in intelligence and it is the
mistake that ruins Isabel. For it is her wealth that arouses Madame
Merle's realization that she can use her and leads directly to the
disastrous, tragic marriage with Osmond. And in the superb scene
in which, sitting in the candlelight in the elegant, spiritually empty
house in Rome, Isabel takes stock of her tragedy, she painfully
reveals to herself the conclusion:

"But for her money, as she saw today, she would never have done
it. And then her mind wandered off to poor Mr. Touchett, sleeping
under English turf, the beneficent author of infinite woe! For this
was the fantastic fact. At bottom her money had been a burden,
had been on her mind, which was filled with the desire to transfer
the weight of it to some other conscience, to some more prepared
receptacle. What would lighten her own conscience more effectually
than to make it over to the man with the best taste in the world?
Unless she should have given it to a hospital there would have been
nothing better she could do with it; and there was no charitable
institution in which she had been as much interested as in Gilbert
Osmond. He would use her fortune in a way that would make her
think better of it and rub off a certain grossness attaching to the good
luck of an unexpected inheritance. There had been nothing very
delicate in inheriting seventy thousand pounds; the delicacy had
been all in Mr. Touchett's leaving them to her. But to marry Gilbert
Osmond and bring him such a portion — in that there would be
delicacy for her as well. There would be less for him — that was
true; but that was his affair, and if he loved her he wouldn't object
to her being rich. Had he not had the courage to say he was glad
she was rich?"[15]

---

[14]Ibid., Chap. XVIII.
[15]Ibid., Chap. XLII.

It is at the moment when Ralph is dying that the theme is finally stated in the form at once the most affecting and most morally profound.

> "She raised her head and her clasped hands; she seemed for a moment to pray for him. 'Is it true — is it true?' she asked.
> 'True that you've been stupid? Oh no,' said Ralph with a sensible intention of wit.
> 'That you made me rich — that all I have is yours?'
> He turned away his head, and for some time said nothing. Then, at last: 'Ah, don't speak of that — that was not happy.' Slowly he moved his face toward her again, and they once more saw each other.
> 'But for that — but for that —— !' And he paused. 'I believe I ruined you,' he wailed.
> She was full of the sense that he was beyond the reach of pain; he seemed already so little of this world. But even if she had not had it she would still have spoken, for nothing mattered now but the only knowledge that was not pure anguish — the knowledge that they were looking at the truth together. 'He married me for the money,' she said. She wished to say everything; she was afraid he might die before she had done so.
> He gazed at her a little, and for the first time his fixed eyes lowered their lids. But he raised them in a moment, and then, 'He was greatly in love with you,' he answered.
> 'Yes, he was in love with me. But he wouldn't have married me if I had been poor. I don't hurt you in saying that. How can I? I only want you to understand. I always tried to keep you from understanding; but that's all over.'
> 'I always understood,' said Ralph.
> 'I thought you did, and I didn't like it. But now I like it.'
> 'You don't hurt me — you make me very happy.' And as Ralph said this there was an extraordinary gladness in his voice. She bent her head again, and pressed her lips to the back of his hand. 'I always understood,' he continued, 'though it was so strange — so pitiful. You wanted to look at life for yourself — but you were not allowed; you were punished for your wish. You were ground in the very mill of the conventional!'
> 'Oh yes, I've been punished,' Isabel sobbed."[16]

The necessity here of stating in its dreadful simplicity the agonizing truth so that the relationship of the two may be purified and deepened shows an intuition the very opposite of sentimental.

---

[16]Ibid., Chap. LIV.

Isabel, then, imagining herself free, has in fact delivered herself into bondage. And the bondage has come about not casually but out of the very force and fortune of her own aspirations to freedom. She has sought life and because she has sought it in this way she has found death.

Freedom, to Isabel and to Ralph (for he has been as much concerned in the issue as she), has been an idealized freedom. They have sought to be free not through a recognition of, but by an escape from, necessity. And in so doing they have delivered Isabel over to an exploitation as crude and more corrupting than the exploitation that would have been her fate if Mrs. Touchett had never visited Albany.

" 'Do you still like Serena Merle?' " is Mrs. Touchett's last question of Isabel.

> " 'Not as I once did. But it doesn't matter, for she's going to America.'
> 'To America? She must have done something very bad.'
> 'Yes — very bad.'
> 'May I ask what it is?'
> 'She made a convenience of me.'
> 'Ah,' cried Mrs. Touchett, 'so she did of me! She does of everyone.' "[17]

The Portrait of a Lady is one of the most profound expressions in literature of the illusion that freedom is an abstract quality inherent in the individual soul.

It is interesting to compare James's book with another great novel written not very long before, *Madame Bovary*, the story of another woman "ground in the very mill of the conventional." It is true that Emma Bovary is, unlike Isabel Archer, not in the least 'fine,' that she fails to escape from her petty-bourgeois social *milieu* and that she is quite incapable of the exalted moral discipline to which Isabel is dedicated, yet we will learn something of James's novel, I think, from a glance at Flaubert's. What is shocking in *Madame Bovary* is the appalling passivity of Flaubert's characters, their inability to fight in any effective way the bourgeois world which Flaubert detests and which relentlessly warps and destroys all fineness in them. The strength of the novel lies in the very ruthlessness of its exposure of romantic attitudes; but therein also lies its weakness, the sense we get of something less than the human

---

[17] Ibid., Chap. LIV.

capacity for heroism, the uneasy suspicions of a *roman à thèse*. *The Portrait of a Lady* gives, as a matter of fact, no more positive response to its revelation of bourgeois values than *Madame Bovary*, yet we do experience a sense of human resilience and dignity. The interesting question is how far this sense — embodied in the 'fineness" of Isabel herself — is merely romantic and illusory.

The issue can perhaps be put in this way: is not the accumulated effect of the novel to present human destiny as inexorably one of suffering and despair? There are a number of tendencies making for this effect. In the first place there is the insistent use of dramatic irony in the construction of the book. Chapter after chapter in the early reaches of the novel is designed to emphasize the fatality facing Isabel's aspirations. The fifth chapter tells us she has come to Europe to find happiness; the sixth that she likes unexpectedness ("I shall not have success (in Europe) if they're too stupidly conventional. I'm not in the least stupidly conventional"). The seventh chapter ends with the following exchange:

> " 'I always want to know the things one shouldn't do.'
> 'So as to do them?' asked her aunt.
> 'So as to choose,' said Isabel."

The eighth draws to a close with

> " 'I shall never make anyone a martyr.'
> 'You'll never be one, I hope.'
> 'I hope not. . . .' "

This is all, it may be argued, simply Henry James at work, extracting from every situation its maximum of point. But the art, it seems to me, is in a subtle sense self-betraying. What is achieved is a kind of inevitability, a sense of Isabel's never standing a chance, which amounts not to objective irony but to the creation of something like an external destiny. Is not martyrdom becoming, in a sense at once insidious and — with all the associations and overtones one may care to give the word — romantic? Is there not to be here a breath — a very sophisticated and infinitely worldly breath — of the emotional and moral inadequacy involved in George Eliot's vision of those latter-day Saint Theresas?

Our final judgement must depend on the climax — the famous ending — of the book. It is from this ultimate impression that we shall have to decide whether James indeed plays fair with Isabel and us, whether he reveals in full profundity and (in the least

cold sense of the word) objectivity a tragic situation or whether
there is a certain sleight of hand, the putting across not of life
but of something which merely for the moment passes for life. But
before we consider this final climax it is worth noting what would
seem an odd weakness in the novel. Is it not a little strange that
of all the essential parts of Isabel's story which are revealed to us
the section of her life most pointedly avoided is that immediately
before her decision to marry Osmond? She has met him, got to
know him somewhat; she then goes away for a year, travelling in
Europe and the Middle East with Madame Merle. When she comes
back to Florence she has decided to marry Osmond. This is, from
the novelist's point of view, the most difficult moment in the book.
How to convince us that a young woman like Isabel would in fact
marry a man like Osmond? And it is a moment which, despite
the revealing conversation with Ralph (which does indeed tell us
something) is, I suggest, not satisfactorily got over. And the point
is that if Isabel's marriage to Osmond is in any sense a fraud
perpetrated upon us for his own ends by the author, the book is
greatly weakened.

At the end of the novel Isabel, after Ralph's death and another
encounter with Caspar Goodwood, returns to Rome. Is her return
to Osmond irrevocable, an acceptance now and for ever of her
'destiny,' or is it tentative, no ending, the situation unresolved?
Mr. F. O. Mattiessen, arguing in the latter sense, has a most
interesting observation:

> "The end of Isabel's career is not yet in sight. That fact raises
> a critical issue about James's way of rounding off his narratives. He
> was keenly aware of what his method involved. As he wrote in his
> notebook, upon concluding his detailed project: 'With strong hand-
> ling it seems to me that it may all be very true, very powerful, very
> touching. The obvious criticism of course will be that it is not
> finished — that it has not seen the heroine to the end of her situation
> — that I have left her *en l'air*. This is both true and false. The *whole*
> of anything is never told; you can only take what groups together.
> What I have done has that unity — it groups together. It is complete
> in itself — and the rest may be taken up or not, later.' "[18]

James's own evidence is of course conclusive as to his intention,
but it is not necessarily relevant as to what is in fact achieved;
and it seems to me that, although the ending of *The Portrait of*

---

[18]*Henry James, The Major Phase* (1946), p. 151.

a Lady does not completely and irrevocably round off the story — the possibility of Isabel's later reconsidering her decision is not excluded — yet the dominant impression is undoubtedly that of the deliberate rejection of 'life' (as offered by Caspar Goodwood) in favour of death, as represented by the situation in Rome. The scene with Goodwood is indeed very remarkable with its candid, if tortured, facing of a sexual implication which James is apt to sheer off. On the whole the effect of this scene, though one understands completely the quality of Isabel's reaction, is further to weight the scales against a return to Rome. Even if Goodwood himself is impossible, the vitality that he conveys is a force to be reckoned with and Isabel's rejection of this vitality involves more clearly than ever the sense that she is turning her face to the wall.

Isabel's return to Rome is certainly not a mere surrender to the conventional force of the marriage vow. The issue as to whether or not she should leave her husband is twice quite frankly broached by Henrietta, as well as by Goodwood. Isabel's first reply to Henrietta is significant:

> " 'I don't know what great unhappiness might bring me to; but it seems to me I shall always be ashamed. One must accept one's deeds. I married him before all the world; I was perfectly free; it was impossible to do anything more deliberate. One can't change that way,' Isabel repeated."[19]

Later, when she discovers how little free she had in fact been, it is her obligation towards Pansy that becomes the most important factor. But always there is the sense of some deep inward consideration that makes the particular issues — the character of Osmond, her own mistakes, the needs of Pansy, the importunity of Goodwood — irrelevant. The recurring image in the last pages is of a sea or torrent in which Isabel is immersed. Goodwood becomes identifed with the torrent. Her temptation is to give herself up to it.* When she breaks loose from him and the image she is once more 'free,' free and in darkness. The lights now are the lights of Gardencourt and now she knows where to turn. "There was a very straight path."[20]

It seems to me inescapable that what Isabel finally chooses is something represented by a high cold word like duty or resignation,

---

*It is at such a moment that one sees the force of Stephen Spender's linking of James with Conrad's "in the destructive element immerse" in an otherwise not very helpful book (*The Destructive Element,* 1937).

[19]*The Portrait of a Lady,* Chap. XLVII.

[20]Ibid., Chap. LV.

the duty of an empty vow, the resignation of the defeated, and
that in making her choice she is paying a final sacrificial tribute
to her own ruined conception of freedom. For Henry James, though
he sees the tragedy implicit in the Victorian ruling-class view of
freedom, is himself so deeply involved in that illusion that he
cannot escape from it. His books are tragedies precisely because
their subject is the smashing of the bourgeois illusion of freedom
in the consciousness of characters who are unable to conceive of
freedom in any other way. His 'innocent' persons have therefore
always the characters of victims; they are at the mercy of the
vulgar and the corrupt, and the more finely conscious they become
of their situation the more unable are they to cope with it in positive
terms. Hence the contradiction of a Fleda Vetch* whose superior
consciousness (and conscience) leads her in effect to reject life in
favour of death. This is a favourite, almost an archetypal situation,
in James's novels. It achieves its most striking expression in *The
Portrait of a Lady* and *The Wings of the Dove* in which another rich
American girl meets, even more powerfully and more exquisitely,
the fate of Isabel Archer.

For James in his supreme concern for 'living' (Milly Theale in
The Wings of the Dove, Strether in *The Ambassadors* have, like
Isabel, this immense, magnificent desire to 'live') ultimately, in
effect, turns his back on life. This is not unconnected, I think,
with the fact that his characters never do anything like work. This
description of Madame Merle is not untypical of a day in the life
of a Henry James figure:

> "When Madame Merle was neither writing, nor painting, nor
> touching the piano, she was usually employed upon wonderful
> tasks of rich embroidery, cushions, curtains, decorations for the
> chimney-piece; an art in which her bold, free invention was as
> noted as the agility of her needle. She was never idle, for when
> engaged in none of the ways I have mentioned she was either reading
> (she appeared to Isabel to read 'everything important'), or walking
> out, or playing patience with the cards, or talking with her fellow
> inmates."[21]

The contemplation of such a way of life is likely, after all, to lead
to idealism, for the necessities behind such an existence are by
no means obvious. It is a superficial criticism to accuse James of

---

*In *The Spoils of Poynton*.
[21]Ibid., Chap. XIX.

snobbery or even of being limited by his social environment (what artist is not?). But there can be no doubt that what the bourgeois world did for James was to turn him into a moral idealist chasing a chimera of ideal conduct divorced from social reality.

It is not that his sense of social reality is in any way weak. On the contrary his picture of his world has, it has already been emphasized, a magnificent solidity, a concrete richness of the subtlest power. Nor is he in any easy, obvious sense taken in by that world (note his attitude to Warburton, his description of American-French society in Chapter XX and his total contempt for Osmond and his values); his picture of European bourgeois life is in its objective aspect as realistic as that of Balzac or Flaubert or Proust. No, if we are to isolate in James's novels the quality that is ultimately their limitation, it is to the core of his point of view, his philosophy, that we are led. The limiting factor in *The Portrait of a Lady* is the failure of James in the last analysis to dissociate himself from Isabel's errors of understanding.

One of the central recurring themes of James's novels is the desire to 'live,' to achieve a fullness of consciousness which permits the richest yet most exquisite response to the vibrations of life. And yet with this need to live is associated almost invariably the sense of death. Living, he seems to be saying again and again, involves martyrdom. The pleasure he finds in the contemplation and description of living at its most beautiful, most exalted point is subtly increased if the living creature is faced with death. Ralph Touchett is not alone among the dying swans of James's books: he is one of a line culminating in Strether (who discovers how to live too late) and in the fabulous Milly Theale. The attraction of this subject to James seems to me most significant. "Very true . . . very powerful . . . very touching . . ." one can almost hear him breathing out the words. It is a kind of apotheosis of his vision of life. And it is intimately, inextricably, linked up with his philosophic idealism. His 'good' characters, in their unswerving effort to live finely, turn out to be in the full implication of the phrase, too good for this world. Their sensibility becomes an end in itself, not a response to the actual issues of life. The freedom they seek turns out to be an idealized freedom; its ends, therefore, can only end, in a desire not merely to be free *in* this world but to be free *of* this world.

The popularity of James's novels among our intelligentsia today is significant too. It includes, I feel certain, not merely a genuine admiration for his extraordinary qualities, but also a powerful element of self-indulgence. It is not only pleasanter but easier to involve oneself in an idealized sensibility, a conscience* removed into realms outside the common and often crude basis of actual living. Many besides Isabel Archer imagine that they can buy themselves out of the crudities through the means of a high-grade consciousness and a few thousand pounds. And Henry James, albeit unconsciously, offers a subtle encouragement. He expresses the fate of Isabel Archer but expresses it in a way that suggests that it has, if not inevitability, at least a kind of glory to it. So that when Isabel takes her decision to return to Rome the dominant sense is not of the waste and degradation of a splendid spirit, but of a kind of inverted triumph. Better death than a surrender of the illusion which the novel has so richly and magnificently and tragically illuminated.

---

*It is interesting to speculate whether Conrad, when he referred to James as "the historian of fine consciences" was using the word in its English sense or with the French implication of 'consciousness.'

Quentin Anderson

From "News of Life"

Many of James's readers, if asked which of his works have most to say about the uncertainties and complexities of the moral life, would doubtless name *The Portrait of a Lady* (1881) and *The Princess Casamassima* (1885).

The Portrait of a Lady and *The Princess Casamassima* are, for different reasons, challenges to any of James's ideas. The first affords his most brilliant presentation of an individual life; and the second makes the fullest and most various uses of the European scene James ever attempted. He tried in each case to exploit a particular mode of achieving novelistic density, and it is a partial measure of his success that these two novels offer more chances for comparison with the fiction of his predecessors and contemporaries than the rest of his major novels. Such studies have been made by F. R. Leavis and Lionel Trilling.[1] Unlike *The Bostonians*, *The Portrait of a Lady* and *The Princess* are clearly written in a mixed

From *The American Henry James* (New Brunswick, N.J.: Rutgers University Press, 1957) pp. 183, 184-98. Reprinted by permission of the publisher.
[1][See Leavis, *The Great Tradition* (New York: George W. Stewart, n. d.), pp. 126-172; and Trilling, "The Princess Casamassima," *The Liberal Imagination* (New York: Viking Press, 1950), pp. 58-92. — EDITOR.]

mode: James's emblematic convention organizes them in part, but
only in part; for the rest, a variety of competing and not altogether
congruous principles are at work.

The question proposed here is this: How do James's "ideas," in
their emblematic form, enter into these works, and to what effect?
Particularly, how is his vision limited or defined by the emblems
described in the preceding chapter? It will be apparent in what
follows that James's powers and his limitations are so interlinked
that we must acknowledge that although the ideas are necessary
conditions of these two novels, they confuse and distort the subjects
James chose to treat.

In both books we may take as a starting point one of the
reflections of its central figure. Hyacinth Robinson asks: "How
can one appear what one is when one is a mixture?"[2] And Isabel
Archer, considering the dangers of inconsistent conduct, decides
that "her life should always be in harmony with the most pleasing
impression she should produce; she would be what she appeared,
and she would appear what she was" (III, 69). The connection
between the situations of these characters which these quotations
suggest is a valid one. Both novels have to do with attempts to
contrive an appearance which will reflect inner reality. But the
perception with which Hyacinth begins his career is the one which
closes Isabel's — we first discover him in the house of life confronted by his antithetical nature, whereas the whole of the novel
which centers about Isabel barely suffices to place her there, and
to make her ask herself whether Mme Merle can be "wicked"
(IV, 329). Since "Madame Merle had married her . . ." (IV, 327),
and she herself had collaborated in the process, some element in
herself must correspond to Mme Merle's wickedness. Emblematically, these novels treat successive stages in our lives. In the first
we fail to see that we are "mixed" until our greed presents us with
an image of ourselves which reveals the other self; in the second
we undertake to celebrate rather than to appropriate the contents
of the house of life.[3] Given these conclusions, let us briefly

---

[2]See also V, 86, 171-172. [Reference is to the "New York edition," Scribners,
1907-1909; subsequent references are to this edition and are usually given
parenthetically in the text. — EDITOR.]
[3]For James's own consideration of the "unfinished" character of *The Portrait
of a Lady*, see *Notebooks*, pp. 15-19; and F. O. Matthiessen, *The Major Phase*,
pp. 173-186. I think it not improbable that James conceived of Hyacinth as a
logical successor to Isabel insofar as his awareness of the European world is
concerned.

recapitulate Isabel's career to see how they may be justified.

We first meet her sitting before the locked outer door of the room known as the "office" in her Albany home. Beyond this door she prefigures "a region of delight or of terror." What she later says of herself at Gardencourt bears out the subtle shading here; the suggestion that the alternatives are exclusive. At Gardencourt, Isabel wonders whether after a childhood so generally pleasant she does not require a certain amount of education through suffering. James reveals in a number of places Isabel's desire to *see* life, without either judging or suffering. This same impulse is seen many times in the desire for the picturesque in James's American travelers — and of course this guilt is common to us all. It is through this delight that terror comes; that we perceive the need of transcending our selfish self and our social self, and arriving at the particular style which frees us from selfhood.

Isabel's experience of terror is long delayed, however. She is in search of that constellation of impressions which will answer to her crystallized desire to be great. Those who seek this image are bound to find it. James makes this very clear by his use of Mme Merle. This lady is not, as Ralph Touchett says, "worldly"; she is "the great round world itself." She is Isabel's fate because Isabel is seeking an account of the world which will minister to her, which will reflect her, as if it were indeed her portrait. "The world" in this emblematic sense is eager to minister to this desire, and Isabel offers in exchange, not simply her beautiful person, her charming spontaneity, but, with Ralph's help, a fortune as well.

This emphasis on Isabel's greed runs quite contrary to our image of her as "spreading her wings," as holding high the torch of possibility, of readiness for moral adventure. Here the doubleness which James later employs to handle the figure of Milly Theale is constantly at work. It is a way of summing up his technical problem in *The Portrait* to say that he must at one and the same time give us this sense of Isabel, which is Ralph's and her own, and also make us aware that her frozen desire must find a frozen complement — that the aim of being "exquisite"[4] which the black Osmond quite honestly proffers is completely congruent with Isabel's own aim as a young woman. The point is that only the self-absorbed person can be trapped by the self-absorbed person;

---

[4]"They [Isabel and Osmond] had attempted only one thing, but that one thing was to have been exquisite. Once they missed it nothing else would do; there was no conceivable substitute for that success" (IV, 247).

and the imagination of greatness can never be the imagination of one's own greatness. Isabel makes a disastrous marriage because she fails to discover "Europe," fails to have the experience of "exaltation and dread" which Brooke has on the Campagna. Isabel evades that relation with something quite "other" which makes for real adventure; with, for example, the steely will of Goodwood, or the fascinating complex of inherited and imposed responsibilities which Warburton's wife would face. Such a relation would, she fears, shatter her image of herself, the portrait of which she is covetous. Down the path indicated by Mme Merle she finds, as she believes, something wholly appropriate to herself, a cup without a flaw into which she can pour her love.

Osmond's proposal makes possible the opening of a long-closed door: "The tears came into her eyes: this time they obeyed the sharpness of the pang that suggested to her somehow the slipping of a fine bolt — backward, forward, she couldn't have said which" (IV, 18). It has been Isabel's notion of happiness that she should realize one of the dreams of her youth; she has done so, the door of the "office" has opened, but, as the figure intimates, she may have made her way into a place of confinement rather than effected her release.

James's use of "portrait" in his title has a double significance. His "lady" makes the mistake which mankind generically makes. She tries to make the world reflect her, instead of perceiving that it reflects the sources of being. At the end of the novel Isabel sets about correcting this error, as we all must. But Osmond's appropriation of Isabel *as* a portrait is an ultimate sin; he tries to make the young American girl, representative of the promise of life, reflect him. He appropriates what might become his conscience. This is not marriage, but concubinage. Isabel's greed is worldly, and corrigible; Osmond's is spiritual, and it damns him. The group of related emblems described in the preceding chapter may of course be applied here. Osmond (whose name suggests something fixed and dead, bony or of the earth) stands at one of the limits of moral motion. When Isabel comes to fear herself, her fear will be of what he represents, absolute or spiritual greed. Having declared at the outset, "I only want to see for myself," she sees Osmond as an image which answers *her* sense of *her* claims on the world. She marries the man who *thinks* he is the first gentleman in Europe. In this way she creates the "blasted circle" (IV, 203) round which she walks, and comes to the realization classic among James's central characters: "I'm afraid," she tells Ralph during their last meeting in Rome, "Afraid of myself" (IV, 306). While she has become afraid, Osmond has become ever more exigent; he holds her on a tighter and tighter rein, since he needs her to reflect him. His prime desire is to "preserve appearances" (IV, 357).

This phrase has for James a weight, a force, which is hard to exaggerate. Those who try to "preserve appearances" at such a cost are trying to preserve false institutional forms which are in deadly opposition to moral spontaneity and the forms to which it gives rise. They represent what the elder James called the "church," an organized inversion of love and truth. Isabel's return to Rome, the house of life in which she has encountered her other self, is emblematically consistent, although it may seem to the reader of the novel to depend too much on an exaggerated idea of the sanctity of marriage, or an exaggerated estimate of Isabel's ability to help Pansy Osmond, who, as the novel presents her, is in a hopeless position.

The novel closes at the moment when Isabel has her foot on the threshold of the adult world. She knows what Maisie knows at the end of the novel in which she figures. She recognizes that one must fear one's own impulses.[5] And something more: All the aesthetic values, all the "old things," the whole burden of the human past which she and Osmond have collaborated in seizing, have now to be reseen, not as possessions, but as evidence of the divine and devilish, of the mixed character of man. She is in the state of the American setting foot in Europe only to exclaim: "Look what I have gone and done!"

Ending the novel here, James leaves on the reader's hands the question of what ultimately happens to Isabel. When she goes back to Pansy, she does not go back to the possibility of action. Pansy is and will remain a hopeless sacrifice to Osmond's respect for "appearances."[6] It is best that she become a nun, for the only alternative is that she be appropriated. Even the elder James is ready to recognize the function of nunneries in Europe. They may save subject women from appropriation.

Since Pansy cannot be helped by Isabel, Isabel's return is a return to the struggle with herself, to the contention with that

---

[5]"She [Maisie] was afraid of herself." (XI, 338; see also pp. 326 and 342.)
[6]See IV, 28, on Pansy's desire to marry her father; and *The Ambassadors*, XXII, 155, for Jeanne de Vionnet's inordinate desire to please Chad Newsome. James's point is explicitly made by D. H. Lawrence; see F. R. Leavis, "The Novel as Dramatic Poem (VII): *The Rainbow*" (*Scrutiny*, XIX, 1952, pp. 16-19).

group of impulses in her of which Osmond is the ultimate expression. James has substituted an emblematic conclusion for a dramatic one. His notebooks suggest that he found this satisfactory, but the book clearly seems more rounded off to him than it can to the uninitiated reader.

The clue to James's moral and symbolic intention at the end of the book is apparent in his description of Isabel's journey northward to see Ralph Touchett, who is dying. Her love for him has led her to make the journey; her awareness of his love for her has been reinforced by Mme Merle's final thrust: Ralph has endowed Isabel with her fortune, Mme Merle tells her. But, just as in the case of Milly Theale and Densher, Ralph's love will be her real inheritance, not the seventy thousand pounds. As she rides, she puts together many memories. The past begins to compose itself into a structure: "The truth of things, their mutual relations, their meaning, and for the most part their horror, rose before her with a kind of architectural vastness" (IV, 391). Even this awareness leaves her passive; she is not ready to do battle with her self.

> Nothing seemed of use to her to-day. All purpose, all intention, was suspended; all desire too save the single desire to reach her much-embracing refuge. Gardencourt had been her starting-point, and to those muffled chambers it was at least a temporary solution to return. She had gone forth in her strength; she would come back in her weakness, and if the place had been a rest to her before, it would be a sanctuary now. She envied Ralph his dying, for if one were thinking of rest that was the most perfect of all. To cease utterly, to give it all up and not know anything more — the idea was as sweet as the vision of a cool bath in a marble tank, in a darkened chamber, in a hot land.
>
> She had moments indeed in her journey from Rome which were almost as good as being dead. She sat in her corner, so motionless so passive, simply with the sense of being carried, so detached from hope and regret, that she recalled to herself one of those Etruscan figures crouched upon the receptacle of their ashes. (IV, 391)

Isabel, with her "sense of being carried" from the scene of her encounter with herself in Rome to her "starting-point," which is now a "sanctuary," reminds us strongly of Brydon in *The Jolly Corner*. She is traversing the path between the same extremes, undergoing a kind of death as she does so. Gardencourt and its fostering love, the Palazzo Roccanera and its image of her selfishness, are in her case the extremities of the "tube or tunnel" of the

Galerie d'Apollon[7] passage. James is at pains to establish her inability, at this stage in her life, to realize fully the meaning of her movement between these extremes.

> Deep in her soul — deeper than any appetite for renunciation — was the sense that life would be her business for a long time to come. And at moments there was something inspiring, almost enlivening, in the conviction. It was a proof of strength — it was a proof she should some day be happy again. It couldn't be she was to live only to suffer; she was still young, after all, and a great many things might happen to her yet. To live only to suffer — only to feel the injury of life repeated and enlarged — it seemed to her that she was too valuable, too capable for that. Then she wondered if it were vain and stupid to think so well of herself. When had it ever been a guarantee to be valuable? Wasn't all history full of the destruction of precious things? Wasn't it much more probable that if one were fine one would suffer? It involved then perhaps an admission that one had a certain grossness; but Isabel recognised, as it passed before her eyes, the quick vague shadow of a long future. She should never escape; she should last to the end. Then the middle years wrapped her about again and the grey curtain of her indifference closed her in. (IV, 392-393)

Isabel's flickering perception of a "certain grossness" in her composition is not a sufficient recognition of the extremes between which mankind moves. Not until the "middle years" have ended is a full recognition of these extremes possible. The important emblematic concept of the "middle years" may be introduced by a quotation from the elder James. His theme here is the familiar one of the need to get over our selfish conviction that appearances are absolute, and may be owned or used to give us moral ascendancy

---

[7] [One of the galleries of the Louvre. In *A Small Boy and Others* (1913), James recounts at length his early experience of the Galerie d'Apollon and its profound influence on him, and later its role in a gripping nightmare — a dream in which he chased a terrifying and at the same time terrified spectre through that gallery. (See *Henry James: Autobiography*, ed. F. W. Dupee [New York: Criterion Books, 1956], pp. 195-200.) Mr. Anderson explains the significance of the passage: "The description of the gallery is a description of the state of innocence; the description of the nightmare is a description of regeneration — the triumphant expulsion of the other self. What lies between these stages is the period of 'the middle years.' " (See *American Henry James*, p. 169.) His point is that James felt the American confronting Europe faced both the best and worst of his own mixed character.

Henry James used the phrase "the middle years" as the title of a short story (1893) and of the third volume of reminiscences, left unfinished at his death (see *Henry James: Autobiography*, pp. 547-599. — EDITOR.]

over others: "Thus, reason emancipated from sense, or what is the same thing enlightened by revelation, disowns our *a priori* reasoning, and pronounces nature an altogether subjective divine work enforced in the exclusive interest of man's spiritual evolution; just as the moral control I exert over myself is a subjective work on my part enforced by my objective regard for society, or my sense of human fellowship; just as an artist's education and discipline — which often are nothing more than his physical and intellectual penury and moral compression — are a needful subjective preparation for his subsequent objective or aesthetic expansion."[8]

The character of childhood as the Henry Jameses conceived of it is a period of innocence in which our "general sense of *glory*" is simply a sense of what our parents, love and wisdom, have provided. There follows a period in which we incur the guilt of appropriating goods and status, or, to put it more generally, as the elder James does above, a period in which we prepare ourselves for "objective expansion." This involves creating a form which is a worthy vessel of the divine love to replace the provisional or "subjective" form. James the novelist frequently uses the term "middle years" to describe a period precisely analogous to what the elder James calls the artist's "subjective preparation." These were the years in which James himself was subject to the provisional delusion that the world can give us a satisfying image of ourselves. In an account in *The Middle Years* of a meeting with certain English celebrities he writes: "My identity for myself was all in my sensibility to their own exhibition."[9]

The "middle years," which James often describes as "grey" (Brydon of *The Jolly Corner* is carried through "an interminable grey passage"), are of their nature obscured by struggle in the world. The attempt to create an identity for oneself out of forms which are not one's own is a long and discouraging process, inspiring feelings of guilt which it has no power to allay. But this process may lead to the great climax of the dream of the Galerie d'Apollon: the acquisition of a form or style powerful enough to banish all guilt. Adam Verver, in considering his "middle time," concludes that "the years of darkness had been needed to render possible the years of light" (XXIII, 144). Such a happy conclusion is not

[8]*Secret*, p. 129. [Reference is to *The Secret of Swedenborg: Being an Elucidation of His Doctrine of the Divine Natural Humanity*, Boston: Fields, Osgood & Co., 1869. — EDITOR.]
[9]See Ferner Nuhn's chapter on James in *The Wind Blew From the East*, p. 105. [(New York: Harper & Brothers, 1942.) — EDITOR.]

foreordained, however, since Strether's "grey middle desert" is not the prelude to a triumph.[10] The artist of the short story called *The Middle Years* comes to accept the loss of his selfhood; he dies into his work, into creation, and his physical end is emblematically a death to selfhood. Nonetheless, there is pathos in his demand for another chance; we listen with sympathy to the outraged cries of the very nearly stifled selfhood demanding a further opportunity to range a world of admirers about its proud identity.

James's use of the term "middle years" to describe the period on which Isabel Archer is entering is an assurance that her life is beginning, not ending. Just at this point, though, there is an imaginative check. We have been given no intimation of the possible creative result which lies ahead. What is Isabel going to do? James has scrambled his moral elements in an odd way.

When we consider the young man of *Travelling Companions*, or Merton Densher of *The Wings of the Dove*, or Prince Amerigo of *The Golden Bowl*, we find that each is exposed to the moral danger of seizing the promise of life in the form of a portrait, a possession, but that it is open to them to subordinate themselves to their spiritual superior: the spontaneous American girl. It is a question of choosing between the two loves, the two ways of taking experience. These young men are posted, in their variously interesting and absorbing ways, between the portrait and the lady. The question is, What will be the direction of their moral motion? Or, to vary the emblems as James does, Will Densher and Amerigo choose the encircling love of Kate and Charlotte, which gives them identity in their own eyes and those of the world, or will they accept the heavy burden of creating an individuality fit to hold the love which multiplies communications and contacts?[11] In these two cases the emblematic elements are discriminable as leading impulses in particular characters, and it is intelligible to say that morally, the action of the novel takes place *within* a character who represents mankind, as do Amerigo and Densher. This mode of rendering a moral career does not, however, help us to classify Isabel's emblematic situation. Certain stories about artists furnish more useful analogues.

In *John Delavoy*, in *The Birthplace*, and in *The Real Right Thing* we may find instances in which a conflict of the sort Densher

---

[10]*The Ambassadors*, XXI, 52. See also XXI, 87, for the phrase "the great desert of the years." For Nick Dormer's "twilight of the soul," see VIII, 267.
[11]*The Tragic Muse*, VII, 148.

and Amerigo undergo is represented by one character, just as
James's account of the Galerie d'Apollon, and of the nightmare of
which it was the scene, sums up the whole of man's struggle in
the house of life. In these three stories, in *The Tragic Muse*, and
in other instances too numerous to name, the moral point is
someone's realization of the difference between the form which
passes current in the world, an identity, and the form which is
associated with creation, spiritual individuality or style. We find
Nick Dormer stating his perception of the difference between
representing a constituency and representing life in this way: "Art
was *doing* — it came back to that — which politics in most cases
weren't" (VIII, 267). Of John Delavoy it is said: "He *was* his
work." And in *The Real Right Thing* the man who has been asked
to undertake a biography of Ashton Doyne is doubtful of the
value of the project because "the artist was what he *did* — he was
nothing else" (XVII, 415). In *The Birthplace* Morris Gedge discovers that the only way to be true to Shakespeare is to stop
making speeches about him as a "person" and start romancing
on his own hook; the only way to be faithful to the meaning of
Shakespeare is to try, no matter how inferior one's instrument, to
celebrate life, instead of appropriating the past. James's sense of
the world simply excludes this possibility for women, however.
Women appear in his work in the guise of the Eve or selfhood
(Kate Croy, Charlotte Stant), in that of the "church," the exist-
ing complex of institutions (Mrs. Newsome, Mrs. Lowder, Mrs.
Assingham), or as the promise of life (the spontaneous American
girl), but never as creators.

Isabel Archer is a changeling, both within the novel in which
she figures and in the Jamesian canon at large. In one respect
she is representative of a stage in the process of refinement which
transformed Minny Temple[12] into Milly Theale; in another, she is
akin to the youthful narrator of *The Author of Beltraffio* or the
young Henry James of *The Middle Years*, an artist who has not
yet achieved his form and tries to borrow it from the world. These
two lines of development intersect in Isabel, whose originals are
Henry James *and* Minny Temple. In short, the reason that the

---

[12] [Mary (Minny) Temple, a cousin of Henry James, was the great love of his
life. She died of tuberculosis in 1870, aged 24, but her memory haunted him
throughout most of his life. She is recognized as being the "original," to some
extent, of Isabel Archer and of Milly Theory ("Georgina's Reasons," 1884),
and expressly by James as the original of Milly Theale in *The Wings of the
Dove*, 1902. — EDITOR.]

ending of *The Portrait of a Lady* is unsatisfactory seems to be that
it is impossible to make Isabel Archer over into a man and launch
her on the career of an artist.

It is possible that in thinking about what might have happened
had tuberculosis been his fate instead of Minny's, James hit upon
the device of making an attenuated James (Ralph Touchett) the
spectator of Minny's (Isabel's) descent upon Europe. Touchett,
sexually impoverished though he is, grants the power which puts
wind in Isabel's sails, gives her life to pursue an imaginary career.
This may help explain James's success in making Isabel seem a
creature wonderfully formed for the highest demands of life. It
may also help to explain why her descent into the valley of the
middle years seems to belie that capacity for life. Like Howells —
who is forever leading his enchanted lovers on a wedding journey
into Canada, down through New England, and then tumbling them
into the drab and unrelieved domesticity of Cambridge — James
simply cannot conceive of a third act for a woman. He tacks
to the career of his transmogrified Minny a promise of artistic
fulfillment; he gives her the pledge that he has given himself: that
he will come through the period of conflict successfully and be able
finally to make an assured and selfless use of his powers. For this
reason Isabel suggests spontaneity and intellectual grace in the
first volume, and a dogged, manly husbanding of creative energy
toward the end of the novel.[13]

Isabel is plainly enough saddled with the burdens of the young
writer who is trying to create a form or portrait out of what the
European world offers, and discovering the error of such an attempt.
The character of Isabel's spontaneity is questioned as well. She is
not really ready to take life in what Gabriel Nash calls the "free,
brave, personal way." In her declaration of principle ("Her life
should always be in harmony with the most pleasing impression
she should produce; she would be what she appeared, and she
would appear what she was.") James indicates Isabel's worst error.
She puts herself at the mercy of "the most pleasing impression"
she has made on others; she proposes to live up to the portrait
instead of the demands of the inner life. What she must learn to
do if she is to become truly spontaneous is to invert the order. She

---

[13]A less hopeful possibility may be imagined. The doleful pre-Raphaelite sister
in *The Author of Beltraffio* opposes "form" to "goodness" in a somewhat
mechanical fashion. The first of these is her brother's forte; the second is his
wife's (XVI, 50-51). She enters a nunnery and dies not long afterwards.

must first of all learn to appear what she *is*. The elder James defines "Spiritual or essential freedom" as "being precisely what one wishes to be, and seeming precisely what one is"[14] Spontaneity of the unqualified sort is exemplified by Milly Theale and Maggie Verver, who possess Minny Temple's extraordinary generosity of spirit, together with a truly personal style which is not dependent on the world's image of them.[15]

Our most immediate sense of the virtues of *The Portrait of a Lady* as a novel depends in part on the way in which Isabel Archer engages the imagination. As a character, she has the authority of existence; her complications and contradictions suggest life. James's powers worked on her in a fashion which, happily, his "ideas" are unable to represent. She is perhaps a study of the Minny Temple one might have known, rather than the Minny Temple of the *Notes of a Son and Brother*.[16] She is high and free and bold in her approach to life; yet James's development of what lies behind this manner leads us to feel that she is ignorant, self-centered, and afraid. In the world of James's later emblematic fictions this would be an anomaly, for in them the complications and contradictions of life are all fully known, fully explicated. But in the tradition of the novel with which F. R. Leavis connects *The Portrait of a Lady* — and in people as we know them — there is nothing in the least incredible in a character whose innocence, ignorance, and self-absorption both charm and alarm us.

James may very well have been intent on producing an American analogue to Emma Bovary, who likewise incorporates internal contradictions. To this end, he would logically make his European scene clear and relatively simple, almost posterish in its broad strokes: Warburton so quintessentially healthy and so proudly seated, the elder Touchett such a beautifully preserved Yankee banker, Osmond so black, Mme Merle so blandly and clearly

---

[14]*Substance*, pp. 431-432. "Spontaneity" is here said to be the "badge" of this freedom. [Reference is to *Substance and Shadow: or, Morality and Religion in Their Relation to Life: An Essay on the Physics of Creation,* Boston: Ticknor and Fields, 1863. — EDITOR.]

[15]The "gross male Adam" tries to impose his will on the world and the woman in order to make them reflect him. Insofar as Isabel does this, she is symbolically "masculine."

Leon Edel argues that James likened women to Diana or Artemis, and notes the connection of the name "Archer" with the divine huntress. This suggests a biographical basis for the novel, and accords with my emphasis on Isabel's masculine quality. (See "Venus and Diana," *The Untried Years*, pp. 252-260.)

[16][The second volume of reminiscences, 1914. See *Henry James: Autobiography*, pp. 239-544. — EDITOR.]

designing, Henrietta Stackpole so merciless and so affectionate — they all seem adjuncts to Isabel's unseeing pursuit of her fantasy. The enchanted lawns of Gardencourt and the grim walls of the Palazzo Roccanera have a storybook quality. The clarity, the light and sure touch, of the prose playing about the figure of Isabel only to reveal an obscurity, a darkness within her lovely presence, has an effect which is among James's greatest achievements. In no other novel does so much of the world's strong light fall on a single person, nor is there any other character in James who could bear this much illumination without becoming emblematically transparent.

The emblematic incoherence of *The Portrait of a Lady*, which makes Isabel a cross between a young woman aspiring to be Milly Theale and a young man aspiring to become an artist, is a piece of good fortune for letters. It is evidence that the "ideas" which haunted James early and late could on occasion give way before "news of life" so haunting and compelling that his need for order had, temporarily, to take second place.

• • •

Lotus Snow

From "The Disconcerting Poetry of Mary Temple: A Comparison of the Imagery of *The Portrait of a Lady* and *The Wings of the Dove*"

Upon the appearance of *The Portrait of a Lady,* published in serial form in the *Atlantic Monthly* during 1880-1881, certain friends of Henry James recognized that Isabel Archer was modeled after Mary (Minny) Temple, his adored cousin who died at twenty-four of tuberculosis. Grace Norton, James's Cambridge friend, wrote to him about the likeness, and he replied, "You are both right and wrong about Minny Temple. I had her in mind and there is in the heroine a considerable infusion of my impression of her remarkable nature. But the thing is not a portrait. Poor Minny was essentially *incomplete,* and I have attempted to make my young woman more rounded, more finished."[1]

To the remarkable nature of Mary Temple, whose death, he felt, marked the end of his youth and his brother William's, James paid tribute many years later in the final chapter of *Notes of a Son and Brother:*

Reprinted from *The New England Quarterly,* XXXI (September, 1958), 312-323, 336-339, by permission of the author.
[1] [From an unpublished letter, quoted in Leon Edel's introduction to the Riverside edition of *The Portrait of a Lady,* p. xv. — EDITOR.]

. . . she was to remain for us the very figure and image of a felt interest in life, an interest as magnanimously far-spread, or as familiarly and exquisitely fixed, as her splendid shifting sensibility, moral, personal, nervous, and having at once such noble flights and such touchingly discouraged drops, such graces of indifference and inconsequence, might at any moment determine. She was really to remain, for our appreciation, the supreme case of a taste for life, as personal living; of an endlessly active and yet somehow a careless, an illusionless, a sublimely forewarned curiosity about it; something that made her, slim and fair and quick, all straightness and charming tossed head, with long light and yet almost sliding steps and a large light postponing, renouncing laugh, the very muse or amateur priestess of rash speculation . . . a disengaged and dancing flame of light.[2]

The image of Mary Temple's suffering — "death, at the last, was dreadful to her; she would have given anything to live" — so struck James as the essence of tragedy that he was, twenty-one years after *The Portrait of a Lady*, to "seek to lay the ghost by wrapping it, a particular occasion aiding, in the beauty and dignity of art."[3] The particular occasion, as he tells us in the preface to the novel, was *The Wings of the Dove*. As the conception of the earlier novel is "a certain young woman affronting her destiny," so the idea of the later is a young person "conscious of a great capacity for life, but early stricken and doomed, condemned to die, under short respite, while enamored of the world; aware moreover of the condemnation and passionately desiring to 'put in' before extinction as many of the finer vibrations as possible, and so achieve, however briefly and brokenly, the sense of having lived."

Further parallels exist between the two novels. In the plots the machinery is almost identical: an American heiress is exploited for her fortune by her best friend and the man of the latter's choice. Milly Theale dies when she learns of the treachery practiced upon her; Isabel Archer, coming to knowledge of her deception by Mme. Merle and Gilbert Osmond, renounces freedom to keep the vows of her impossible marriage. Both girls play out their dramas in munificent theatres: Rome and Venice. Each is provided with a Jamesian confidant, her cousin Ralph Touchett for Isabel, and for Milly her companion Susan Stringham. A significant difference between the two novels occurs, however, in the characters of the

---

[2] [See *Henry James: Autobiography*, p. 283. James's phrase is "dancing flame of *thought*," rather than "of light." — EDITOR.]
[3] [*Autobiography*, p. 544. — EDITOR.]

male fortune-hunters. Milly's Densher has been enriched with a conscience. Indeed, with the closing chapters of *The Wings of the Dove* the tragedy becomes Densher's, for it is he who undergoes the regeneration of the hero of classic drama.

As well as in the heightening of Densher's character, James's preoccupation with the theme of betrayal reveals itself in the growth of his imagery between the two novels. Since any mention of a modern author's imagery has come to imply his knowledge of Freud, Sir James Frazer, and their successors, it may be well to mark here the boundaries of James's usage. In his discussion of *The Wings of the Dove*, F. O. Matthiessen has pointed out the delimitations of James's imagery. Although he was aware of the French movement, he was not a symbolist. Unlike the symbolist poets and, later, Proust and Thomas Mann, he was not concerned with the suggestiveness of music; his analogies were all with painting, drama, and literature. Further, he did not live to become conscious of the possibilities of dealing with the symbols of either Freudian psychology or of anthropology, as T. S. Eliot and Virginia Woolf were to do. Rather, James uses imagery in the older tradition of poetic drama, "to give concretion, as well as allusive and beautiful extension, to his thought." How richly James's imagination reworked the theme of betrayal in the twenty-one years between *The Portrait of a Lady* and *The Wings of the Dove* is evidenced by his recurrent use in the latter of thematic imagery sufficient in itself to carry his meaning. To compare the imagery of the two novels whose "germ" was Mary Temple's tragedy is to compare James's youthful and his mature vision of the qualities of life.

I

In planning the structure of *The Portrait of a Lady*, James reviewed Turgenev's practice of allowing a story to originate in a character or characters, as well as George Eliot's belief that an interesting young woman as heroine can carry a story. Taking courage from the success of their theories, he determined to build a story from his vision of "a particular engaging young woman." The usual device of a novelist for showing the worth of his heroine is to provide the other characters with occasions for attesting it. James utilized this device, but he made it contributive to a resource he thought more convincing, the testimony of the young woman herself. Accordingly, he made Isabel Archer's consciousness the central recorder of the novel. She engages in a steady scrutiny of her relation to herself as it is affected by others, and the others contribute their impressions of her.

As a result of this design, imagery in the novel serves the functions of characterizing the *dramatis personae* and their relationships. The nature of a young woman capable of affronting her destiny is first to be established, of course, and Isabel, as primary recorder, is given many pages of self-analysis. James uses a recurrent image for her relation to herself. This image, military in origin, shows her as initially the commander of her own forces. Her mind she thinks a vagabond and she has

> ... spent much ingenuity in training it to a military step and teaching it to advance, to halt, to retreat, to perform even more complicated manoeuvres at the word of command.

She is not accustomed to keeping her imagination "behind bolts" and, "ridiculously active,"

> when the door was not open it jumped out the window.

She is "very liable to the sin of self-esteem":

> ... she often surveyed with complacency the field of her own nature; she was in the habit of taking for granted, on scanty evidence, that she was right; she treated herself to occasions of homage.

And yet she recognizes the danger of a high spirit,

> ... the danger of keeping up the flag after the place has surrendered; a sort of behavior so crooked as to be almost a dishonor to the flag. But Isabel, who knew little of the sorts of artillery to which young women are exposed, flattered herself that such contradictions would never be noted in her own conduct.

Introspection is, after all, "an exercise in the open air." Armed with such equipment as a fine mind, imagination, a high spirit, and introspection, she sees her destiny as

> a swift carriage, of a dark night, rattling with four horses over roads that one can't see.

When, in the early days of her intimacy with Mme. Merle, the latter defies life to spoil Isabel, she

received this assurance as a young soldier, still panting from a slight
skirmish in which he has come off with honor, might receive a pat
on the shoulder from his colonel.

The interlude after Daniel Touchett has left her a fortune and
before she meets Gilbert Osmond is "a hush in the drum and fife"
of her career, and here the military imagery of the first volume
stops. It is resumed two years after Isabel's marriage as she envies
Mme. Merle's apparent absence of feeling, her seeming to live by
reason and wisdom:

> . . . it was a pleasure to see a character so completely equipped for
> the social battle. She carried her flag discreetly, but her weapons
> were polished steel, and she used them with a skill which struck
> Isabel as more and more that of a veteran.

Isabel has become increasingly aware of "the advantage of being
like that" — of having made one's self a firm surface, "a sort of
corselet of silver."

Significantly enough, the final image of the military sequence
occurs in the chapter James regarded as the finest in the book,
the chapter of Isabel's midnight vigil, in which the reader is made
fully aware of the misery of her marriage. Though she cannot see
her husband's traditions as superior, she is no longer a commander,
but rather a captive, and

> . . . she nevertheless assented to this intimation that she too must
> march to the stately music that floated down from unknown periods
> in her husband's past; she who of old had been so free of step, so
> desultory, so devious, so much the reverse of processional.

The picture of Isabel as a captive is further extended by the
recurrent image of her as a winged creature. As she contemplates
Lord Warburton's proposal, she realizes that it is not compatible
with her idea of herself as freely exploring life and "moves back
into the deepest shade" of the opportunity, "even as some wild,
caught creature in a vast cage." Caspar Goodwood, in making her
his proposal, "had never supposed she hadn't wings and the need
of free beautiful movements." When, finally, she accepts Gilbert
Osmond's proposal, her cousin Ralph tells her that she is "caught,"
she will be "put in a cage"; she had seemed to him to be "soaring
far up in the blue," and now she "drops to the ground" for "a faded
rosebud, a missile that should never have reached" her. After her
marriage, she looks to Lord Warburton like "a winged creature

held back." And Isabel herself, recognizing that "her poor winged spirit had always had a great desire to do its best," wishes not to blame Mme. Merle for making her marriage. To do so "might feed her sense of bitterness, but it would not loosen her bonds."

Another recurrent image of Isabel's need for liberty is the likeness of her to a ship. When Ralph Touchett persuades his father to leave her half his inheritance, he explains that he would like "to put a little wind in her sails," "to see her going before the breeze." Again, as Ralph's mother worries that Isabel is capable of marrying Osmond for the beauty of his opinions or for his autograph of Michael Angelo, Ralph reassures her, "She may have slackened speed for an hour, but before we know it she'll be steaming away again." Upon leaving Rome, the scene of her courtship by Osmond, Isabel reflects "that happy things don't repeat themselves, and her adventure wore already the changed, the seaward face of some romantic island from which, after feasting on purple grapes, she was putting off while the breeze rose." In the key chapter of Isabel's midnight vigil, she recognizes that she had married Osmond out of a kind of romantic, if misguided, tenderness: "He was like a sceptical voyager strolling on the beach while he waited for the tide, looking seaward yet not putting to sea. It was in all this she had found her occasion. She would launch his boat for him. . . ." Caspar Goodwood, however, is no mere voyager needing his boat launched; he is a ship in his own right, and Isabel recalls her telling him that she has accepted Osmond as "a collision of vessels in broad daylight. There had been no mist, no hidden current to excuse it, and she herself had only wished to steer wide. He had bumped against her prow, however, while her hand was on the tiller, and — to complete the metaphor — had given the lighter vessel a strain which still occasionally betrayed itself in a faint creaking." In the closing pages of the novel after Isabel has defied Osmond, to sit at Ralph Touchett's deathbed, Goodwood comes to Gardencourt to implore her to leave Osmond and come with him. The world seems to poor Isabel "to take the form of a mighty sea, where she floated in fathomless waters" and Caspar as help come in a "rushing torrent." But as he kisses her and she realizes the kiss as an act of possession, she thinks of "those wrecked and under water following a train of images before they sink."

One other recurrent image is used about Isabel, and this one has to do with the familiar question of what so remarkable a girl will do with herself. It is an image of which James is very fond, here and elsewhere, an image of keys. With his mother's bringing

Isabel to Gardencourt, Ralph Touchett feels that the key of a beautiful edifice has been thrust into his hand and he told to walk in and admire.

> He surveyed the edifice from the outside and admired it greatly; he looked in at the windows and received an impression of proportions equally fair. But he felt that he saw it only by glimpses and that he had not yet stood under the roof. The door was fastened, and though he had keys in his pocket he had a conviction that none of them would fit.

In the second usage Isabel draws back in alarm from her candour with Mme. Merle:

> It was as if she had given a comparative stranger the key to her cabinet of jewels. These spiritual gems were the only ones of any magnitude that Isabel possessed, but there was all the greater reason for their being carefully guarded.

Gilbert Osmond also uses the figure in a playful moment of courtship:

> 'I'm perfectly aware that I myself am rusty as a key that has no lock to fit it. It polishes me up a little to talk with you — not that I venture to pretend I can turn that very complicated lock I suspect your intellect of being!'

When he has turned the lock, when Isabel realizes that she cares for him, tears come to her eyes, and the sharpness of her feeling "suggested to her somehow the slipping of a fine bolt — backward, forward, she couldn't have said which."

In Isabel's circle of friends, no one else speaks as constantly in metaphor as Ralph Touchett does, a gift befitting the role of detached and amused observer which his condition of advanced pulmonary disorder has led him to adopt. Only one recurrent image is used about Ralph, but the wealth of single images all build to it: generous spectatorship at the game of life and particularly at Isabel's drama. Nor have the images about any other character, not even Isabel, the tenderness of those lavished on Ralph. Shuffling across the lawn at Gardencourt, his hands in the pockets of his brown velvet jacket, he introduces himself as being of no more use, in his mother's opinion, "than a postage stamp without gum." Then James lifts him up into a crescendo of imagery. Once Ralph was aware of the condition of his lungs, "a secret hoard of indifference — like a thick cake a fond old nurse might have slipped into his first school outfit — came to his aid and helped to reconcile him to sacrifice"; "living as he now lived was like reading a good book in a poor translation — a meagre entertainment for a young man who felt that he might have been an excellent linguist"; "his serenity was but the array of wild flowers niched in his ruin." As Ralph tells Isabel, he keeps a band of music in his ante-room:

'It has orders to play without stopping; it renders me two excellent services. It keeps the sounds of the world from reaching the private apartments, and it makes the world think that dancing's going on within.'

Ralph never divests himself of the "loose-fitting urbanity that wrapped him about like an ill-made overcoat." He makes the state of his health seem an intellectual advantage:

Blighted and battered, but still responsive and still ironic, his face was like a lighted lantern patched with paper and unsteadily held.

Even as he lies dying, his face is "strangely tranquil": it is "as still as the lid of a box."

Every image describing Gilbert Osmond and his relations to others alludes to art as opposed to nature. He "suggested, fine gold coin as he was, no stamp nor emblem of the common mintage that provides for general circulation; he was the elegant complicated medal struck off for a special occasion." He looks to Mme. Merle "like a demoralized prince in exile"; to Ralph "like a prince who has abdicated in a fit of fastidiousness and has been in a state of disgust ever since"; to his sister, the Countess Gemini, "as if he believes himself descended from the gods"; and to Isabel "as fine as one of the drawings in the long gallery above the bridge of the Uffizi." For Isabel his speech is "the vibration of glass," and he utters his ideas as if they were "old polished knobs and heads and handles, of precious substances, that could be fitted if necessary to new walking-sticks — not switches plucked in destitution from the common tree and then too elegantly waved about." His taste alone he consults in everything, "as a sick man consciously incurable consults at last only his lawyer." Indeed, it is his taste that has made his daughter Pansy "a precious work of art," "the ideal *jeune fille* of foreign fiction," "a blank page," "the small winged fairy in the pantomime," "the white flower of cultivated sweetness," "an infanta of Velasquez," "a nosegay composed all of the same flower," or, as Mrs. Touchett contends, an insipid little chit.

During his courtship of Isabel he believes that she is "a polished, elegant surface" which will reflect his thought; that her intelligence will be "a silver plate, not an earthen one — a plate that he might heap up with ripe fruits, to which it would give a decorative value, so that talk might become for him a sort of served dessert"; that he "could tap her imagination with his knuckles and make it ring." Or, as Isabel later sees, what he had intended was that "her mind was to be his — attached to his own like a small garden-plot to a deer-park. He would rake the soil gently and water the flowers; he would weed the beds and gather an occasional nosegay. It would be a pretty piece of property for a proprietor already far-reaching."

What he thinks of Isabel after a year of marriage, his hatred of her independence of imagination, we learn only in her account during her midnight vigil. In this chapter images of darkness and suffocation abound. For Isabel, her life with Osmond is "a dark, narrow alley with a dead wall at the end"; a corridor in which Osmond has "deliberately, almost malignantly, put out the lights[4] one by one"; "the house of darkness, the house of dumbness, the house of suffocation" with "an odour of mould and decay." Ralph's little visit to Rome is "a lamp in the darkness." Osmond, "his egotism hidden like a serpent in a bank of flowers," is, as Ralph had warned Isabel, a sterile dilettante.

Images to characterize Mme. Merle all pertain to worldliness. Possessed of "a sort of world-wide smile, a thing that over-reached frontiers," she is always described as "smooth," "round and replete," "too flexible, too useful, too ripe, and too final." She likens herself to a porcelain pot, "shockingly chipped and cracked," but "cleverly mended." Isabel senses in her "values gone wrong, or as they said at the shops, marked down." Ralph sometimes feels almost sorry for her because "she had got herself into perfect training but had won none of the prizes"; she is only "almost as universally 'liked' as some new volume of smooth twaddle." As for Osmond, "he seldom consented to finger, in talk, this roundest and smoothest bead of their social rosary." After the Countess Gemini has revealed to Isabel that Serena Merle and Gilbert Osmond had been lovers for seven years, that Pansy is Mme. Merle's child as well as his, and that Mme. Merle made Isabel's marriage for Osmond and their daughter, Isabel meets her at the convent where Osmond has imprisoned Pansy. Her presence there has to Isabel "all the character of ugly evidence, of handwritings, of profaned relics, of grim things produced in court." Mme. Merle is not, as Ralph puts it, "merely worldly": "She's the great round world itself!"

---

[4] [James's phrase is "put the lights out one by one." — EDITOR.]

Very few images are expended on Lord Warburton whose handsome importance is sufficiently conveyed by large substantives. He has "the air of a happy temperament fertilized by a high civilization"; a "radiance of good feeling and good fare surrounded him like a zone of June weather"; he keeps every one of his merits — "properties these partaking of the essence of great decent houses, as one might put it; resembling their innermost fixtures and ornaments, not subject to vulgar shifting and removable only by some whole break-up"; his friendship is to Isabel "like having a large balance at the bank."

On Isabel's other suitor, Caspar Goodwood, the straight young man from Boston, a quantity of military imagery is used to show the aggressive masculinity that at once explains Isabel's ambivalent reactions toward him and his undaunted perseverance in passion for her. Isabel likes to believe "that he might have ridden, on a plunging steed, the whirlwind of a great war"; she sees "the different fitted parts of him as she had seen, in museums and portraits, the different fitted parts of armoured warriors — in plates of steel handsomely inlaid with gold." When, in London, she rejects his proposal, his eyes seem to her "to shine through the vizard of a helmet," and she reflects that "he might always be trusted to dress his own wounds," because he is "naturally plated and steeled, armed essentially for aggression." On his first visit to Florence to hear from Isabel's own lips that she is to marry Osmond, he is "straight, strong and hard"; on his second, two years later, to see for himself whether she is happy, he is still "perpendicular," going straight ahead "with a face like a February sky." At Gardencourt in the closing pages of the novel his love for Isabel is likened to a great natural force: the hot wind of the desert, a rushing torrent, white lightning. Across the novel Isabel rejects him five times, but the rejections are accompanied by fits of weeping or "vibration like the humming of a smitten harp."

Images for the minor characters provide *The Portrait of a Lady* with much of the gaiety that is almost entirely absent from *The Wings of the Dove*. Isabel's friend Henrietta Stackpole, journalist for the American *Interviewer*, is, to Ralph, "as crisp and new and comprehensive as a first issue before the folding," with "no misprint" and yet "not in large type and horrid headings." She smells of the Future enough to knock one down. She has ocular surfaces that glitter, and she flashes lanterns into people's souls. People are collections of good or bad material to her; even the Englishman she finally concludes to marry is to her "as clear as the style of a good prospectus." Isabel's eccentric and literal aunt, Mrs. Touchett, is "as honest as a pair of compasses"; the "edges of her conduct have a knife-like effect." Her husband, Daniel Tracy Touchett, one of the most appealing characters in the novel, has "a fine ivory surface." Pansy's little suitor Ned Rosier always smells of heliotrope, and the Countess Gemini is a tropical bird, attired in shimmering plumage, perched upon twigs, and uttering her remarks "with a series of little jerks and pecks, of roulades of shrillness."

•   •   •

III

Very few of the single or recurrent images of character and relationship in *The Portrait of a Lady* are repeated in the thematic imagery of *The Wings of the Dove*. The images depicting Mme. Merle's worldliness, the sense she gives Isabel of values marked down, suggest the marketplace imagery. Again, the image of Mme Merle traveling with Isabel to Athens and Constantinople, "a lady-in-waiting to a princess circulating *incognita*," seems directly to foreshadow the fairy-tale imagery. Although Ralph Touchett's image of Isabel as a ship recurs throughout the *Portrait*, it is like the extensive sea imagery of *The Wings of the Dove* only in Susan Stringham's initial comparison of Milly's nature to a big boat. Significantly, Isabel is a sailing ship; Milly is a great steamer resembling a leviathan. There is, of course, no dove imagery in the *Portrait* unless Isabel as a winged creature can be correlated with Milly's wondrous wings.

However, a number of the images of *The Portrait of a Lady* reappear in *The Wings of the Dove* apart from the thematic imagery. The military imagery in which Isabel conceives both herself and Caspar Goodwood is repeated in Kate's relation to Aunt Maud Lowder and in Milly's view of the martial posture she adopts to face her doom. The image of keys, used by Ralph, Osmond, and Isabel herself, occurs to Susan Stringham in four instances in which she comes to know more about Milly's "case." The journalistic imagery in which Ralph hilariously characterizes Henrietta Stackpole recurs in a sober version in Densher's mind. For example, he sees himself initially as "but a sentence, of a sort, in the general text, the text that . . . showed as a great grey page of print that somehow managed to be crowded without being 'fine.' " Again, Kate is to him "an uncut volume of the highest, the rarest quality": he does not choose to "read the romance of his existence in a cheap edition." Interestingly, too, an image that James was greatly to expand in his characterization of Prince Amerigo of *The Golden Bowl* is used with both Osmond and Densher, an image of a coin. Osmond is a "fine gold coin," "an elegant complicated medal struck off for a special occasion"; Densher's elements, "the metals more or less precious, are so in fusion and fermentation that the question of the final stamp, the pressure that fixes the final value, must wait for comparative coolness."

Imagery in the two novels reflects their relative complexity of structure. All the characters of *The Portrait of a Lady* are capable of expressing themselves and their relationships in images. Osmond possesses a wealth of them drawn from his *objets d'art* and designed to deprecate the vulgarity of society. Mme. Merle tactfully plucks them in abundance from her large experience of the world. Even Mrs. Touchett is not altogether incapable of imagery, though she deplores her son's "allegorical way of speaking." Ralph does indeed appear to be the character most addicted to metaphor, so much occasion has he had to cultivate the art. But actually it is Isabel in whose consciousness the greatest number of images occur. Like the rest of her cast, Ralph speaks his images, in fulfillment of the function of testifying to Isabel's interestingness. Isabel thinks hers, in keeping with James's design that her intelligence operate as his primary recorder.

Equally in accord with the muted presentation of Milly is the fact that the three groups of thematic images which elaborate the contrast of spiritual and material values in *The Wings of the Dove* do not originate with her. Kate, as representative of London society, is responsible for the marketplace imagery; Susan Stringham, as the romantic daughter of the Puritans, for the fairy-tale; and Kate again, as a character who grows from grace to corruption, for the dove. Milly rapidly grasps the double implication of each of the three groups and quietly capitalizes upon it, putting her wealth to the uses of the spirit, the princess, and the dove. Only the sea imagery originates with her, and, since her whole animus is her desire to live, there is an exquisite appropriateness in her use of the imagery which represents life itself. As for Susan's use of sea imagery, she is, like Ralph Touchett with Isabel, the finely sensitive and devoted confidante, sharing the very quality of her young woman's thought. Like Milly, Densher learns all the patterns of imagery, but only that of the sea is his own. Throughout the novel he refuses to use the fairy-tale and the dove imagery, insisting that Milly is to him only the little American girl. Kate's marketplace imagery fascinates him, "the mastery of her mere way of putting things" seeming to him part of her capacity for life. But at the close of the novel he does call Milly a princess and a dove, and he is chilled, appalled, at the marketplace imagery. The sea imagery is always his, as it is Milly's, because he too deeply experiences betrayal, loss, and renunciation. The closeness in relation of James's four primary recorders enables him to elaborate his theme with infinite subtlety and depth.

The Wings of the Dove is a grimmer and a richer book than *The Portrait of a Lady*. In the early novel the single and recurrent images characterizing Isabel Archer's fortune-hunters and their relationships present the baseness of exploitation. Osmond's imagery is unrelievedly black; Mme. Merle's is tempered by a show of her motives and of her suffering. Except for the two adventurers, however, imagery in *The Portrait of a Lady* reveals the prevalence of good — in Ralph Touchett's generous spectatorship, in Lord Warburton's largeness of nature and Caspar Goodwood's steely fidelity, in the honest eccentricities of Mrs. Touchett and Henrietta Stackpole, above all in Isabel's high imagination of "beauty and bravery and magnanimity." In the late novel the four groups of thematic images underline indelibly the far-reaching power of evil against the small, steady force of good. The imagery of the marketplace discloses the profit motive as the very basis of society, not merely the English society of Bagehot's Victorian Compromise, but Vanity Fair itself. The highly sophisticated use of naïve fairy-tale imagery gives the immemorial conflict of folklore a bitter twist: the fair princess triumphs over her dark sister only in death. The Christian imagery of the dove deepens Kate's wickedness and Densher's redemption, even as it lights Milly's goodness. Finally, the imagery of the sea universalizes the journey of Milly and of Densher from innocence to experience.

James's artistic journey in the years between the novels indicates the extent to which his mind reworked the idea of betrayal. Isabel Archer is betrayed by her imagination; Mme. Merle and Gilbert Osmond are but the agents of its romantic flights. In reality she betrays herself. But Milly Theale is betrayed by her body and by her goodness. Kate betrays her, and her response is not renunciation, as Isabel's is, but death. Whether, as Graham Greene speculates, Mary Temple's death impressed James with the sense of life's treachery, of the betrayal of hope, we cannot know.[5] More probable, perhaps, is the correspondence of James's observation with Mary Temple's experience, so that when, early and late, he came to clothe in fiction his own knowledge, an image for it, forever radiant in his memory, awaited him.

---

[5] [See Greene, "The Portrait of a Lady," *The Lost Childhood and Other Essays* (London: Eyre and Spottiswood, 1951), pp. 40-44; also "Henry James: The Private Universe," *ibid.*, p. 25. — EDITOR.]

Leon Edel

The Portrait of a Lady

The Portrait of a Lady was the third of Henry James's large studies of the American abroad and twice as long as either of its predecessors. In *Roderick Hudson* he had posed the case of the artist, the limitations of his American background, and the frustration of his creative energy from the moment it was confronted by passion. In *The American* he had pictured an ambitious business-man, bent on civilizing himself, proud enough to know his worth, and arrogant enough to think that the best of Europe was none too good for him. *The Portrait* was envisaged as a kind of feminine version of *The American,* and James began with the thought that his Isabel Archer would be a female Christopher Newman. Indeed this may be why he named her Isabel; there is a certain logic in moving from Christopher to the Queen who sent him faring across the ocean. And Isabel Archer deems herself good enough to be a queen; she embodies a notion not unlike that of Isabella of Boston, whose motto was *C'est mon plaisir.*[1]

From Henry James: *The Conquest of London, 1870-1881* by Leon Edel. Copyright © 1962 by Leon Edel. Published by J. B. Lippincott Company. Reprinted by permission of the author's agent, William Morris Agency, Inc., and J. B. Lippincott Company.

[1][Isabella Stewart, who married Jack Gardner of Boston, became a famous hostess and patroness of the arts. The young Bernard Berenson was enlisted to recommend and buy pictures and *objets d'art* for her; and her home, the Venetian palazzo on the Fenway, is now the Gardner Museum of Boston. James met "Mrs. Jack," as she was called, in 1879. — EDITOR.]

In Isabel Archer, Henry wished to draw "the character and aspect of a particular engaging young woman," and to show her in the act of "affronting her destiny." Like her male predecessors she goes abroad a thorough provincial, with her "meagre knowledge, her inflated ideals, her confidence at once innocent and dogmatic, her temper at once exacting and indulgent." A person who is dogmatic and exacting on the strength of meagre knowledge can only be characterized as presumptuous; and there is presumption in Isabel, for all the delicacy of her feeling: presumption suggests also a strong measure of egotism. James presents her to us as a young romantic with high notions of what life will bring her; and also as one who tends to see herself in a strong dramatic light. She pays the penalty of giving "undue encouragement to the faculty of seeing without judging"; she takes things for granted on scanty evidence. The author confesses that she was "probably very liable to the sin of self-esteem; she often surveyed with complacency the field of her own nature." He speaks of her "mixture of curiosity and fastidiousness, of vivacity and indifference, her determination to see, to try, to know, her combination of the desultory flame-like spirit and the eager and personal creature of her conditions." And he adds: "She treated herself to occasions of homage."

The allusion to her "flame-like spirit" suggests that Isabel images Henry's long-dead cousin Minny Temple, for he was to describe her in the same way. He was to confess that he had actually thought of Minny, in creating the eager imagination and the intellectual shortcomings of his heroine. But Minny, as he pointed out to Grace Norton, had been "incomplete." Death had deprived her of the trials — and the joys — of maturity. Henry, as artist, could imagine and "complete" that which had been left undone. Nevertheless, if Isabel has something of Henry's cousin in her make-up, she has much of Henry himself. He endows her, at any rate, with the background of his own Albany childhood, and as in *Washington Square* he interpolates a section wholly autobiographical, depicting his grandmother's house, the Dutch school from which he himself had fled in rebellion (as Isabel does), the "capital peach trees," which he had always sampled and always remembered. The scene is re-evoked years later in the autobiographies.

The most Jamesian of Henry's heroines is thus closely linked by her background and early life to her creator. And when Henry sends Isabel to Europe and makes her into an heiress, he places her in a predicament somewhat analogous to his own. Henry was hardly an "heir"; but his pen had won him a measure of the

freedom which others possess through wealth. In posing the questions: what would Isabel do with her new-found privileges? where
would she turn? how behave? he was seeking answers for himself
as well as for her. The questions are asked in the novel by Ralph
Touchett, Isabel's cousin, a sensitive invalid who has silently
transferred his inheritance to her. He knows he has not long to
live; and he wishes to see how Isabel's large nature will profit by
endowment. If this is a sign of his love for her, and the sole way
in which he can be symbolically united to her, it is also Ralph's
way of living vicariously in Isabel's life and participating in whatever fate her temperament may reserve for her. He, too, has a
substantial fund of egotism.

Like her early predecessor in *Watch and Ward*, Isabel presently
finds herself with three suitors. The first is a young man of very
respectable fortune and family, from the United States, who has
pursued her abroad. His name is Caspar Goodwood. He is an individual who has a "disagreeably strong push, a kind of hardness
of presence, in his way of rising before her." He insists "with his
whole weight and force." He is in short monotonously masculine;
and if Isabel finds his sheer sexual force attractive it is also terrifying. Passion, or sex, as with Roderick, is not freedom. She rejects
Goodwood several times during the novel and flees from him at
the end when she finds his kiss to be like "white lightning." When
"darkness returned she was free."

The second suitor is less dull and much less terrifying. He is a
British lord named Warburton, a fine upstanding liberal, without
too much imagination, one of the types Henry has met at his club
or in country houses, fortunate heir of a position in a hierarchical
society and the substantial means by which to sustain it. He
inspires a different kind of fear in Isabel. "What she felt was that
a territorial, a political, a social magnate had conceived the design
of drawing her into the system in which he rather invidiously lived
and moved. A certain instinct, not imperious, but persuasive, told
her to resist — murmured to her that virtually she had a system
and an orbit of her own." Social position in a word was also
not freedom; moreover, social position in a hierarchical society
represented a strong threat to a woman powerful enough and
egotistical enough to believe that she has "an orbit of her own."

Isabel is romantic, and young. "I'm very fond of my liberty,"
she says early in the book, and she says also, "I wish to choose my
fate," quite as if the ultimate choice were hers. If we see this as
containing a measure of the egotism of youth, we must recognize

that in her case it has its ingenuous charm. Nevertheless Henrietta Stackpole, an energetic and rather meddlesome newspaperwoman, recognizes it for what it is — for she is endowed with not a little egotism herself. She reminds Isabel: "You can't always please yourself; you must sometimes please other people."

At this stage Henry's heroine is still full of her hopes and dreams. Asked to define success — a matter of some interest to her author — she replies that it is to see "some dream of one's youth come true." And asked to define her idea of happiness she offers a vision of a journey into the unknown — "A swift carriage, of a dark night, rattling with four horses over roads that one can't see." The concept is largely that of a girl who reads novels. However, the young lady from America does not really mean what she says. She tries very hard to see, at every turn, the roads before her — and in broad daylight. She is supremely cautious in action, for one so daring in her fancy. And what she discovers is that even in daylight on a clear highway, it is possible to take a wrong turning.

Isabel's wrong turning occurs without her knowledge, when she meets a woman of a certain age who is worldly-wise and accomplished, the last word in refinement, an American expatriate of long standing, who has absorbed Europe into her being and bestrides the Continent with that appearance of freedom and insouciance to which Isabel aspires. The charm she exhibits, the deep attraction Isabel feels for her, are founded in part on the girl's inexperience of people and her inability to recognize the treacheries of life. The woman's name is Madame Merle. The *merle* is a blackbird.[2] Serena Merle introduces Isabel to another American expatriate, who lives in a thick-walled villa in Florence on Bellosguardo, with his young daughter. At this point Henry places in his novel his early vision of Francis Boott and Lizzie, recorded in his travel sketch of 1877, when he had mused on the "tranquil, contented life" of the father and daughter, and the exquisite beauty that was a part of their daily existence. He had spoken of Frank and Lizzie as "figures in an ancient, noble landscape," and Gilbert Osmond and his daughter Pansy are such figures. Pansy, though pictured at a younger age than Henry had ever known Lizzie, is re-imagined as having the same cultivated qualities of the *jeune fille*, the *achieved* manners of an old civilization. Osmond, however, bears no resemblance to

---

[2*Merle* figures in various uncomplimentary French expression, which James undoubtedly knew, such as *un fin merle* (a cunning old bird), *un vilain merle* (a dirty dog), and *un merle blanc* (a rare bird, lit. a white crow). — EDITOR.]

Boott, who was an open, generous, naïve and easy-laughing amateur of life. Osmond's sinister character derives from other sources, and in all critical speculation as to who was his "original," the principal original has been overlooked. To discover him we must compare him first with Catherine Sloper's father in *Washington Square*. He has the same intelligence and the same piercing sarcasm. As a father, Osmond is capable of the same coldness to his daughter's feelings. But he is an infinitely more malign father, and his will to power is infinitely greater than Dr. Sloper's self-aggrandizement in the Square.

"There were two or three people in the world I envied," Osmond tells Isabel shortly after meeting her, "— the Emperor of Russia, for instance and the Sultan of Turkey! There were even moments when I envied the Pope of Rome — for the consideration he enjoys." Nothing less than the Tsar of all the Russias, and the man who could claim to be holier than all others. We grant Osmond his fine irony, as he says this, but we must nevertheless recognize what it expresses. Since he cannot be Tsar or Sultan or Pope, Osmond has consoled himself with being "simply the most fastidious young gentleman living." By now he is no longer young; he is confirmed, however, in his own private domain of power, as the perfect collector of bric-à-brac and *objets d'art*, and a subtle manipulator of persons as well as things. Pansy has been made into one of these objects: and Isabel is to be added to the collection. Strange as it may seem, Osmond clearly expresses one side of Henry James — the hidden side — not as malignant as that of his creation, but nevertheless that of the individual who abjures power by clothing it in meekness and deceptive docility. In this sense, Henry is the "original" of his villain. Osmond is what Henry might, under some circumstances, have become. He is what Henry could be on occasion when snobbery prevailed over humanity, and arrogance and egotism over his urbanity and his benign view of the human comedy. Perhaps the most accurate way of describing this identification with Osmond would be to say that in creating him Henry put into him his highest ambition and drive to power — the grandiose way in which he confronted his own destiny — while at the same time recognizing in his villain the dangers to which such inner absolutism might expose him. In the hands of a limited being, like Osmond, the drive to power ended in dilettantism and petty rages. In Henry's hands the same drive had given him unbounded creativity.

Isabel and Osmond are then, for all their differences, two sides of the same coin, two studies in egotism — and a kind of egotism which belonged to their author. For Isabel, generous high-minded creature though she is, in pursuit of an abstraction she calls "freedom," insists self-centeredly (in spite of grim warnings from all her friends) that she has found it in Osmond. She sees "a quiet, clever, sensitive, distinguished man . . . a lovely studious life in a lovely land . . . a care for beauty and perfection." He is the "elegant complicated medal struck off for a special occasion" and she feels it to be her occasion. Has she not always felt she was rather "the special thing" herself — a subject of her personal homage? And now, possessed of her wealth, it is as if she could combine her own power with the quiet existence of this individual and his exquisite flower-like daughter. When she marries him she believes that it is she who brings powerful elements into the union: "she would launch his boat for him; she would be his providence." This is indeed an exalted notion of her role, and it suggests the role she assigned to Osmond. Thinking back on this later, she wonders at the "kind of maternal strain" she had possessed in her passion; she believes that her money had been her burden. But this is rationalized after the fact. Isabel and Osmond had been attracted to one another because each saw in the other a mirror-image of self. The two had experienced an irresistible need for each other and in the end they cannot suffer each other. Power may be attracted to power, but it cannot endure it. Each insists on supremacy. Osmond tries to bend Isabel to his will. She cannot be bent. Her kind of power refuses to be subjugated: it exerts its own kind of subjugation. His, more devious, returns perpetually to the assault. The impasse is complete.

Henry had written into this work two aspects of himself: there was his legitimate aspiration to freedom, and his covert drive to power hidden behind his compliance, docility and industry. In the largest sense, egotism and power are the real subjects of *The Portrait of a Lady*, concealed behind a mask of free will and determinism. How was one to possess the power and arrogance of one's genius and still be on good terms with oneself and the world? How was one to establish relationships with people when one felt — and knew — one was superior to them? Yet how avoid loneliness and isolation? Above all, how enjoy one's freedom and not make mistakes in the exercise of it? Ralph watches Isabel make her mistakes: and it is he who in the end delivers the uncomfortable verdict that she has been "ground in the very mill of the conventional." Ralph thereby accepts Isabel at her own evaluation; he believes, as she did, that she was worthy of something more than the conventional. And beyond the unhappiness of Isabel's marriage lies the revelation that she has been the victim of a carefully-laid plot: that Madame Merle had been the mistress of Osmond; Pansy is their child; and the marriage had been arranged by the wily "blackbird" to endow Pansy with Isabel's fortune.

It is possible in this light to see that Isabel's rejection of Goodwood and Warburton went beyond the mere sense that they threatened her freedom. They would have inhibited her freedom to exercise her power. Goodwood would have imposed his masculinity and the power of his passion; Warburton would have involved Isabel in a society where the determinants of power had been fixed long before. She had looked upon one aspect of herself in Osmond and had fallen in love with it. He had done the same in looking at her. The other image, that of Osmond's selfishness and his "demonic imagination," belong in all probability to Henry's "buried life," some part of which he concealed even from himself, but which emerged from the depths in the writing of this character.

In *The Portrait of a Lady* there is a kind of continuous endowment of the characters with aspects of their author and the questions arising in his life even as he was writing the book — as if he were putting on different hats and different neckties and looking at himself in a series of mirrors. Curiously enough this observation was made long before the biographical knowledge we possess today enables us to identify this process of character infiltration. James Herbert Morse, writing in the *Century Magazine* a year after the publication of the novel, observed that there was in nearly every personage of *The Portrait* "an observable infusion of the author's personality." He went on:

> The men and women are almost equally quick-witted, curt and sharp. While each has a certain amount of individuality, the sharpness is one of the elements in common, preventing a complete differentiation. It is not wit alone, and repartee, but a sub-acid quality which sets the persons to criticising each other. One does not like to call it snarling. Mr. James is too much of a gentleman to admit snarling among ladies and gentlemen; and yet every leading person in the book does, in a polite way, enter frequently into a form of personal criticism of somebody else.[3]

------

[3] [James H. Morse, "The Native Element in American Fiction Since the War," *Century*, XXVI (July, 1883), 362-375, esp. 372 ff.; quotation is from p. 373. — EDITOR.]

Since Morse wrote these lines we have come to understand the technique by which James sought to cover up what he was doing; his method of using shifting angles of vision so as to make us feel the way in which people see one another. We see Osmond through the eyes of all the principal characters, and this dramatizes even more Isabel's blindness to his faults during the period when she is debating whether she will marry him. Morse was right, however, in feeling that in a certain sense the various speakers in the novel were "engaged in the business of helping the author develop his characters." On the level of technique, this was one of James's brilliant devices: and later he was even to boast that he created artificial characters for this purpose and managed to endow them with the attributes of life. For biography, however, this method has the unusual effect of throwing a personal shadow behind the impersonal puppets projected and fashioned by the artist's imagination. "We cannot escape the conviction," said Morse, "that he has at least so far written himself into his books that a shrewd critic could reconstruct him from them." And he went on to be the shrewd critic: "The person thus fashioned would be one of fine intellectual powers, incapable of meannesses; of fastidious tastes, and of limited sympathies; a man, in short, of passions refined away by the intellect."

This needs amendment today. The visage of the writer reflected in *The Portrait* is rather that of a man of large sympathies and powerful passions, which are in some degree inhibited, and which are struggling to be set free, indeed which are using all kinds of indirection to find some liberating channel. And it is in the relationship between Isabel and Osmond that we can best observe this at work.

In the end one feels that Isabel's disillusionment, the damage to her self-esteem and the crushing effect of her experience, reside in the shock she receives that so large a nature should have been capable of so great a mistake; and in her realization that instead of being able to maneuver her environment, as her freedom allowed, she had been maneuvered by it. Christopher Newman had had a similar shock, in the Faubourg St. Germain. But he could write it off as the corruption and deceit of the French nobility. The deeper illusion here resides in the fact that Serena Merle and Gilbert Osmond are Americans, and the implications are that as expatriates, long divorced from their native soil, they also have been corrupted: they conceal a world of evil unknown to Isabel. America had ill prepared her for this. The American and the Americana, in

Henry's two novels, represented — in the larger picture — the New
World's concept of its own liberties, the admixture of freedom and
of power contained in America's emerging philosophy, and in the
doctrines of pragmatism of which Henry's brother William was to
be a founder. In drawing his novel from the hidden forces of his
own experience into the palpable world of his study and observation, Henry James had touched upon certain fundamental aspects
of the American character.

When he had sent off his early instalments, Henry received certain worried letters from Howells. The editor suggested that Isabel
was being over-analyzed; and that the figure of the American newspaperwoman, Henrietta Stackpole, was overdrawn. "In defense of
the former fault," Henry replied, "I will say that I intended to
make a young woman about whom there should be a great deal to
tell and as to whom such telling should be interesting; and also
that I think she is analysed once for all in the early part of the
book and doesn't turn herself inside out quite so much afterwards."
This, in the end, was not to be true; Henry was to consider the
book's finest passage to be Isabel's self-analysis after she perceives
the relationship between Madame Merle and Gilbert Osmond. As
for Miss Stackpole, Henry told Howells that she was not "I think
really exaggerated — but 99 readers out of a 100 will think her so:
which amounts to the same thing. She is the result of an impression
made upon me by a variety of encounters and acquaintances made
during the last few years; an impression which I had often said to
myself would not be exaggerated."[4] Henry however added that perhaps it was an impression which "the home-staying American"
would not receive as vividly as the expatriate. "It is over here that
it offers itself in its utmost relief."

It is possible to discover one "original" for Miss Stackpole in
Henry's letters. Shortly after he had moved to London, William
sent to him a young woman from Cambridge, a Miss Hillard
(probably the Katherine Hillard who edited her mother's journal
and later an abridgement of Madame Blavatsky's doctrines). Writing to William on June 28, 1877, Henry says: "I have got to go
and see your — excuse me but I must say — accursed friend Miss
Hillard, who has turned up here and writes me a note every three
days, appointing an interview. I do what I can; but she will certainly tell you that I neglect her horribly. Do you admire her, particularly? She is, I suppose, a very honorable specimen of her type;
but the type — the literary spinster, sailing-into-your-intimacy-

---

[4] [Letter of 5 December 1880. — EDITOR.]

American-hotel-piazza type — doesn't bear somehow the mellow light of the old world. Miss H. announced her arrival here to me by writing to ask me to take her to the Grosvenor Gallery and Rembrandt etchings and then go out and dine with her — at Hammersmith miles away! — at the Conways'! And this a maid whom I had never seen!" Henry then interrupted this letter to call on Miss Hillard and on returning added: "I have in the interval of my two sentences driven over to the remote region of Paddington and back, at an expense of three shillings, to see Miss H. whom I did not find. But she will nevertheless deem that I have neglected her."

On the back of this letter, in William's hand, are the following words: "Do you notice the demoniac way in which he speaks of the sweet Miss Hillard?" Decidedly Miss H. had impressed the brothers quite differently. In a letter a few days later Henry added to the chronicle of his adventures with Miss H. "I did what I could further about Miss Hillard, who has left London: called again upon her and saw her, and went to a party at the Boughtons' in order to meet her." He added: "She is a good girl: her faults are that she is herself too adhesive, too interrogative and too epistolary. I have received (I think) seven notes and letters from her, for two or three that I have written her."[5] The final mention of her occurs in a letter some weeks later, when Henry says to his mother of William: "His silence has led me to fear that he is 'mad' at what I wrote touching poor dear Miss Hillard; if so I take it all back."[6]

If he took it back, he nevertheless had found his type. And Henrietta Stackpole, her forthrightness, good humor, meddlesomeness, and hundred-per-cent Americanism, in the *Portrait* was to be but the first of a number of characterizations of the gossipy American journalist abroad. Miss Stackpole is able to say all the things Goodwood, in his supreme inarticulateness, does not utter. She is completely characterized in an interchange between Isabel and Ralph. "She's a kind of emanation of the great democracy — of the continent, the country, the nation," Isabel says. And Ralph replies: "She does smell of the Future — it almost knocks one down."

A great deal has been made of the resemblance of *The Portrait of a Lady* to *Daniel Deronda*. As *Roderick* had been Henry's conception of the novel Hawthorne might have written about Rome, so *The Portrait* was Henry's way of making Isabel Archer the personality he felt George Eliot should have made of Gwendolen Harleth. His description of Gwendolen, in his dialogue on the Eliot novel, can be

---

[5] [Letter of 10 July 1877. — EDITOR.]
[6] [Letter of 4 September 1877. — EDITOR.]

applied to Isabel. Henry had written that she "is a perfect picture of youthfulness — its eagerness, its presumption, its preoccupation with itself, its vanity and silliness, its sense of its own absoluteness. But," he added, "she is extremely intelligent and clever, and therefore tragedy *can* have a hold upon her." And again: "The universe forcing itself with a slow, inexorable pressure into a narrow, complacent, and yet after all extremely sensitive mind, and making it ache with the pain of the process — that is Gwendolen's story."[7] It is Isabel's as well. She is indeed the victim of her own complacent temperament, and the real determinism of the novel is psychological determinism. If *The Portrait of a Lady* can be related to George Eliot's novel (and the character of Grandcourt related to Osmond), the work Henry wrote is still pure James, and the distillation of his own experience, his fierce will to freedom as an artist, his hidden fear of his drive to power, his awareness that, no matter how careful one may be, one can still be betrayed by one's own egotism.

Over and above its substance *The Portrait of a Lady* established itself, by degrees, as one of the best-written novels of its age. In a prose of high style, with a narrative unsurpassed for its rhythmic development, with a mastery of character and of all the threads of his complicated story, Henry had created a novel that could be placed among the supreme works of the century. It introduced into a Europe that was reading Turgenev and Flaubert, and would soon be reading Tolstoy, a distinctly American heroine.

Her portrait hangs in the great gallery of the world's fiction. We can see Isabel as we saw her when she first stepped into the garden of the Touchetts, at Gardencourt; her clasped hands are in repose, they rest in the lap of her black dress. She looks at us with her light gray eyes, and her face, framed by its black hair, possesses a distinctive American beauty. She holds her head high; she possesses a great pride, and there is something arrogant in her steady gaze.[8] The gallery in which Henry placed her was remarkable. On its walls were the paintings of many other women who, like Isabel, had never literally "lived." All of them were tissued out of the minds of their authors, mere figments of the literary imagination, creatures of the printed word. And yet they all had taken on a life

---

[7] [See "Daniel Deronda: A Conversation," *Atlantic Monthly*, XXXVIII (December 1876), 684-694; reprinted in *Partial Portraits* (1888). — EDITOR.]
[8] [Mr. Edel may possibly have had in mind Frank Duveneck's portrait of Lizzie Boott (1880), now in the Cincinnati Art Museum. Lizzie Boott became Mrs. Frank Duveneck in 1886. — EDITOR.]

of their own — Becky Sharp, or Dorothea Brooke, the Lady of the Camellias or Jane Eyre, Anna Karenina or Emma Bovary. It was as if they had really lived. And Isabel Archer, who partakes of this reality, and who actually seems to have resided in Albany, and ultimately in a palace in Rome, retains her uniqueness among her European sisters. Theirs had been largely dramas of love, often of physical passion. Isabel's had been a drama of suppressed passion, passion converted into high ideals and driven by a need for power that reckoned little with the world's harsh realities.

The painting is exquisite. Every touch of the artist's brush has been lovingly applied to his subject who, though not a daughter of the Puritans, has something of their rigidity in her bearing and not a little of their hardness of surface. She looks down at us always in the freshness of her youth — and the strength of her innocence and her egotism.

Tony Tanner

The Fearful Self:
Henry James's
The Portrait of a Lady

I

The feeling which Isabel Archer most consistently experiences is fear. She is frightened by Warburton's offer, of Caspar Goodwood's persistence, and Gilbert Osmond's anger; she is frightened of sexual passion, of her unexpected wealth, of her 'freedom'; but beneath all these specific apprehensions there is, she admits, a deeper, radical fear — fear of herself. Seeing that it is a self which can misread Osmond so disastrously and make such a profoundly mistaken choice then, we may say, she has good grounds for her fear. But her fear, her error, and her final resolution are, it seems to me, crucial stages on a psychic journey which forms the very heart of the novel. This journey is the journey of an uncommitted, undefined self which sets out to find the right house to live in and the right partner to live with. A house — because the undefined self needs a defining shape: a partner — because the self can only realise what it is, by seeing itself reflected in the chosen and respected eyes of another; in selecting a partner it is selecting the gaze and regard which will assure it of its own reality and value. Putting it very

Reprinted from *The Critical Quarterly*, VII (Autumn, 1965), 205-219, by permission of the author.

crudely, Isabel Archer chooses the wrong house and the wrong partner. It is the full nature of this error — and her subsequent actions — that I wish to explore. But first I should like to make it clear that if I tend to treat characters, events and buildings as being 'emblematic' (Quentin Anderson's word),[1] this does not mean that I am insensitive to the more realistic qualities of the novel which are praised, for example, by F. R. Leavis in *The Great Tradition*. I certainly do not wish to suggest that the book is something aridly schematised and drained of the opaque complexity of life in the interests of abstract meanings. The life is there: Isabel remains a hauntingly authentic and elusive character moving through vivid and tangible territories. But James has so selected and arranged his realistic data, and has so saturated it with deeper implications, that Isabel's journey is also an analogue of the journey of the inquiring self seeking realisation and identity. Everyone she meets, every house she enters, all are detailed, plausible, recognisably of the world. But they are also significant steps of an inward quest which far transcends the social realism of a young American girl living in late nineteenth century Europe. In this essay I shall be stressing the inner quest more than the outer realism — but of course, either without the other would be an immeasurably poorer thing. To suggest the full significance of Isabel's error I shall be considering some of the characters and then some of the architecture. But first I want to make a general point about the Jamesian world which I can best clarify by introducing a quotation from Kant (not, indeed, suggesting any direct influence, even though Henry James Senior studied Kant fairly thoroughly). Kant asserts that 'in the realm of ends everything has either a value or a worth. What has a value has a substitute which can replace it as its equivalent; but whatever is, on the other hand, exalted above all values, and thus lacks an equivalent . . . has no merely relative value, that is, a price, but rather an inner worth, that is, dignity. Now morality is the condition in accordance with which alone a reasonable being can be an end in himself, because only through morality is it possible to be an autonomous member of the realm of ends. Hence morality, and humanity, in so far as it is capable of morality, can alone possess dignity'. This idea is compactly summarized in his second categorical imperative. 'So act as to treat humanity, whether in thine own person or in that of any other, in

---

[1] [See the passage from Anderson's *The American Henry James* included in this collection, above, pp. 67-79. — EDITOR.]

every case as an end withal, never as a means whereby.' And this key statement was probably influenced, as Ernst Cassirer has suggested, by Rousseau's maxim: 'Man is too noble a being to serve simply as the instrument for others, and he must not be used for what suits them without consulting also what suits himself . . . . It is never right to harm a human soul for the Advantage of others'.

I have introduced these quotations because I think they offer useful terms with which to outline James's moral universe. Imagine two worlds. One is the world of ends in which everything and everyone has an intrinsic worth and they are all respected for what they are. That is, literally, they are regarded as ends in themselves. This is the moral world. In the other world, everything and everyone is regarded as a means, nothing is considered as having a fixed inherent worth but only what Kant calls a 'value'. This is misleading since we tend to use 'value' to imply 'worth', so let us say 'price' i.e. a market value which may change as appetites change, as opposed to an inner spiritual value, a permanent immutable worth. In this lower world of means, people only look at each other in the light of how they can use people, manipulate them, exploit or coerce them in the interests of some personal desire or appetite, or indeed mutilate and shape them to fit the dictates of a theory or a whim. In this world people see other people as suits their own ambition. The world of means is a world of rampant egoism, while the world of ends is the realm of true morality and love. These two worlds are effectively the upper and lower parts of James's moral world. And what happens to Isabel Archer is that while she thinks she is ascending towards the world of ends, she is in fact getting more deeply involved in the world of means. The shocking knowledge she has to confront after her marriage is that she is "a woman who has been made use of" as the Countess Gemini puts it. She who thought herself so free, so independent, a pure disciple of the beautiful, now has to face up to the 'dry staring fact that she had been an applied hung-up tool, as senseless and convenient as mere shaped wood and iron'. She, of all people, finds herself trapped in the world of instruments and things. Seeking a world of disinterested appreciation, she falls into a world of calculating appropriation. How does an error of such magnitude come about?

II

Isabel Archer's character has been amply analysed by many other critics so all I want to do is stress that from the outset her approach to life is very romantic, idealistic, and theoretic. 'Isabel Archer was a young person of many theories; her imagination was remarkably active' as James tells us clearly enough. And Henrietta Stackpole is certainly correct when she says to Isabel: "The peril for you is that you live too much in the world of your own dreams". What these dreams consist of we know right from the start: 'she spent half her time in thinking of beauty and bravery and magnanimity; she had a fixed determination to regard the world as a place of brightness, of free expansion, of irresistible action . . . she was always planning out her development, desiring her perfection, observing her progress'. Thus, she views the world as a benevolent sphere which will be plastic to her theories of 'free expansion' and 'irresistible action'. She seems unprepared for any harsh encounter with all that indifferent otherness which is not the self, which is not amenable to the self, and which may well prove cruel and hostile to the self. More dangerously, it is hard to see how she intends to put her theories of self-development into practice. What will that expansion and action consist of? As we soon realise, her most characteristic response in the real world is one of refusal and rejection. Like many another character in American fiction much of her energy goes into avoiding any commitment which might serve to define and arrest her. She is generally in favour of 'the free exploration of life' and yet she shrinks from any of the solid offers that life holds forth. Caspar Goodwood suggests oppression, coercion and constraint on the plain physical level. Lord Warburton with his complex social relations and obligations suggests immobilisation on the social level. If she rejects the first out of a distinct disinclination to enter a firm physical embrace, she rejects the second on 'theoretic' grounds because what he offers does not tally with her vague notions of indefinite expansion. So we may say, summing up, that she rejects the physical and the social in her theoretic pursuit of freedom, knowledge, and self-realisation. Why, then, does she go on to accept Osmond? As she realises, 'The world lay before her — she could do whatever she chose' — the Miltonic echo is deliberate, it recurs again. And out of the whole world to choose Osmond! Notice that she is the only character in the book who is remotely taken in by this 'sterile dilettante' as Ralph so cogently calls him. Why? When we first see her she is reading a history of German thought; that is to say, drinking from the very source of American transcendentalism. And when, later, she imagines her future married life with Osmond, she feels assured of 'a future at a high level of consciousness of the beautiful'. This implies a sort of romantic Plato-

nism which she might well have found in her youthful reading. She
wants to exist at the heights of sheer communion with ideal beauty.
As opposed, we may say, to involving herself with the lower levels
of un-ideal actuality, From the start she tests things and people
by whether they please her 'sublime soul'; and when she receives
her fortune, the vast amount of money gives her 'to her imagination, a certain ideal beauty'. Isabel's instinct for the actual is as
curtailed as her longing for the ideal is exaggerated. She rejects the
sexual and social life. In marrying Osmond she thinks she is embracing the ideal. She idealises herself, her motives for marrying,
her ambitions, and Osmond himself. It is all pathetically wrong.
But as Mrs. Touchett shrewdly says: "there's nothing in life to
prevent her marrying Mr. Osmond if only she looks at him in a
certain way". Looking at him in her own way — romantically, the-
oretically (she 'invented a fine theory about Gilbert Osmond'),
consulting her yearning for a life lived on the ideal level — Osmond
seems perfectly suited to Isabel's needs.

Among other things, then, her mistake is the result of a radical
failure of vision: idealising too much, she has perceived all too
little. But more than that, Osmond is exactly what a large part of
Isabel wants. He seems to offer release from the troubling life of
turbulent passions; he seems to offer a life dedicated to the appreciation of ideal beauty. As we well know, Osmond merely regards
Isabel as worthy 'to figure in his collection of choice objects'; but
consider how Isabel feels about herself just before her marriage and
at the height of her confidence in herself: 'she walked in no small
shimmering splendour. She only felt older — ever so much, and as if
she were "worth more" for it, like some curious piece in an anti-
quary's collection'. And she enjoys this feeling. It is hard to resist
the conclusion that a part of her — the theorising, idealising part
— is quite prepared to be placed in Osmond's collection. The lady
is half willing to be turned into a portrait. And, given her temperament, there is much to be said for becoming a work of art. It offers
a reprieve from the disturbing ordeals awaiting the self in the mire
of the actual. Osmond is a student of the 'exquisite' and we discover how cruel and sterile that can be. But in her own way so is
Isabel. She speaks honest words about their marriage: 'They had
attempted only one thing, but that one thing was to have been
exquisite'. In some ways Osmond is as much a collaborator as a
deceiver.

Although there are hints of the proper villain about Osmond
(James perhaps goes a little too far by revealing that Osmond's

favourite author is Machiavelli), he is in fact a curiously hollow, insubstantial man: "no career, no name, no position, no fortune, no past, no future, no anything" as Madame Merle says. Perhaps this apparent lightness, this seemingly empty detachment from the world is more attractive to Isabel than the solid identity, the heavy actuality of Goodwood and Warburton. Certainly his claim that he has renounced passional life and ordinary human attachments to pursue this high-minded study, his 'taste', echoes something in Isabel. The paradox, of course, as Ralph sees, is 'that under the guise of caring only for intrinsic values Osmond lived exclusively for the world. Far from being its master as he pretended to be, he was its very humble servant, and the degree of its attention was his only measure of success'. He pretends to be a devotee of the ideal, to have renounced the base world. This is what draws Isabel. But to care so totally and uncritically for forms, taste, convention ("I'm convention itself" he revealingly admits) is to be absolutely enslaved to mere appearances, never questioning essences or the intrinsic worth of things. This, precisely, makes him a dedicated inhabitant of the world of means. He has renounced the lived life of instinct and action not, like Ralph, the better to appreciate its intrinsic values, but in order to give himself over entirely to calculated surface effects. How far he will take this is of course revealed by what he does to his daughter Pansy. It is the same thing as what he wants to do to Isabel — to turn her into a reflector of himself, utterly devoid of any spontaneous life of her own. Isabel of course, having stronger and richer stuff in her, can resist. But Pansy shows the process all but complete. All her natural vitality and spontaneity have been quietly suffocated to be replaced by a perfected puppet-like behaviour which does not *express* Pansy's own inner life, but simply *reflects* Osmond's taste. Such a total appropriation of another person's life for egotistical ends is of course the cardinal Jamesian sin. But there is something in Isabel herself which is not so remote from Osmond's disposition. At one point we read that she was 'interested' (a neutral word) to watch Osmond 'playing theoretic tricks on the delicate organism of his daughter'. She should be interested, for she has spent her whole life playing theoretic tricks on her own organism. Osmond is an egotist, but so, we are told, is Isabel: he is cold and dry, but so is she: he pays excessive attention to appearances rather than realities, and up to a point so does she (I will return to this): he prefers art to life, and so does she: he has more theories than feelings, more ideals than instincts, and so does she. He is a collector of things, and she offers herself up to him as a fine finished object. Isabel accepting Osmond's proposal of marriage is the uncertain self thinking it is embracing the very image of what it *seeks* to become. Her later shock and revulsion is the self discovering the true worthlessness of what it might have become. Osmond is Isabel's anti-self. This is why, I think, James made Osmond American when he might well have made him a cynical European ensnaring American gullibility. He is American because Isabel is American. She of course has qualities which differentiate her sharply from Osmond. But she also has tendencies which draw her straight to him. He is an actualisation, a projection, of some of the mixed potentialities and aspirations of her questing, uncommitted self. He is part of her self writ large, and when she learns to read that writing properly (she actually refers to not having 'read him right'), she is not unnaturally appalled.

I must here say a little about the other American 'parasite' and plotter, Madame Merle. As Osmond is 'convention itself' so she is 'the great round world itself'. She is totally devoted to the world of things—she thinks of it in terms of 'spoils'—and she has subjected the unruliness of authentic nature to the surface perfection of contrived manner. Isabel is not so blind as not to be able to detect her occasional cruelty, her subtle dishonesty, the sense she gives of 'values gone wrong'. But unlike Osmond, there is something pathetic about her, and something which also offers a warning to Isabel. For clearly Madame Merle was, like Isabel, first used and then abused by Osmond, and she has not gained anything from the world even though she has devoted herself to it. She keeps herself going by 'will', forcing, always, the right mask for the right occasion. But she ends up utterly dried up, unable to cry: "you've dried up my soul" she says to Osmond (it is worth recalling here that no less a writer than Shakespeare habitually depicted evil as a state of dessication, a complete lack of the very sap and tears of life). Perhaps the saddest cry in the whole novel is Madame Merle's lament: "Have I been so vile for nothing?" It at least attests to a vestigial moral sense which she has deliberately subverted for the world's ends, only to see no gains. She has been a disciple of appearances and indeed has mastered the art, but she is rewarded by being banished to America (apparently the worst fate James could conceive of for an erring character). She is a sadder case than Osmond because she knows that she is doing bad things to Isabel. Her effects are as calculated as Osmond's but at least she winces at perpetrating them. She is an almost tragic example of the scant rewards and plentiful shames awaiting those who live only for 'the world'. And it is Madame Merle who gives perhaps the most succinct expression of living in the world of means to be found in the whole book. "I don't pretend to know what people are for" she says, "I only know what I can do with them". She exactly fits Kant's (and Rousseau's) definition of the immoral world. She sees people as instruments but has no sense of their intrinsic worth: means to her hand, not ends in themselves.

In the world of Osmond and Madame Merle, self-seeking and simulation go together. They have to calculate effects: what *is*, is neglected; what *seems* is paramount. Now Isabel herself is a partial devotee of appearances. I will quote a few references to this. She has 'an unquenchable desire to please' and 'an unquenchable desire to think well of herself': thus she is "very liable to the sin of self-esteem'. More subtly, we read of 'her desire to *look* very well and to *be* if possible even better'. A similar crucial distinction is made later: Isabel's chief dread 'was that she should *appear* narrow-minded; what she feared next afterwards was that she should really *be* so'. (My italics in both cases.) These fine hints reveal a problem of great importance for the novitiate self: which will receive more attention — appearance, or essence? For much of the early part of her travels Isabel falls into the subtle and understandable error of devoting herself to appearances. She wishes to emulate Madame Merle. She contrives to appear to Osmond as she thinks he wants her to appear; like a fine finished work of art which re-echoes and reflects his ideas and taste. In this sense Osmond *is* a man deceived, and Isabel is right to realise that she did mislead him by appearing to be what in fact she was not. That is why Isabel has a true instinct when she says she is afraid of herself. Realising the depths of her error with regard to Osmond is also to realise that she does not know what her self is, nor what it may do. (After all there is Madame Merle, a terrible example of how the self may mutilate the self from a sense of misplaced devotion and ambition.) And indeed this is the crucial difficulty for the self. Only by engaging itself in a situation, projecting itself into the world of things and appearances, can the self realise the self (i.e. transform latent potentialities into visible realities). But once in that situation, it may find that it has chosen a position, a role, which falsifies the self. We don't know what is in us until we commit ourselves in a certain direction: then we may find that the commitment is utterly wrong. Thus all choice may turn out to be error and in this way the self may ruin the self. Certainly Isabel exacerbates her chances of choosing wrong by coldly consulting her theories, her imaginative ideals, her book-fed romanticisms; and that wrong choice does seem to threaten years to come of waste and disappointment. Seen thus, Isabel's difficulty, her error, her fate, form a journey on which we must all, in our different ways, go. For it is only through choice and commitment that we can find out what we are. In this sense error is also discovery. Isabel has to close with Osmond in order to arrive at a deeper knowledge of her self, of her distorted values, of her egotism, and of the real pain and cruelty of life. By marrying Osmond she suffers in good earnest, but she thus earns the right to see the ghost of Gardencourt. Her consolation — and it is the supreme one in James — is truer vision.

III

To bring out more clearly Isabel's journey as the journey of the developing but all-too-often erring self, I now want to move from the characters she meets to the buildings and settings she moves through. And first I must quote from a crucial exchange between Isabel and Madame Merle: it comes near the end of chapter nineteen and is really central to the whole book. Talking of an earlier suitor Isabel says: "I don't care anything about his house" and Madame Merle replies: "That's very crude of you. When you've lived as long as I you'll see that every human being has his shell and that you must take the shell into account. By the shell I mean the whole envelope of circumstances. There's no such thing as an isolated man or woman; we're each of us made up of some cluster of appurtenances. What shall we call our 'self'? Where does it begin? Where does it end? It overflows into everything that belongs to us — and then it flows back again. I know a large part of myself is in the clothes I choose to wear. I've a great respect for *things*. One's self — for other people — is one's expression of one's self: and one's house, one's furniture, one's garments, the books one reads, the company one keeps — these things are all expressive".

Now this idea that the self is only the self that we consciously create and play at being, the self that we visibly express and project, is still being explored by existential psychologists like Sartre (for instance in *Being and Nothingness* where he discusses the waiter 'playing at being a waiter . . . the waiter in the cafe plays with his condition in order to *realize* it'), and by such imaginative sociologists as Erving Goffman (his brilliant book *The Presentation of Self in Everyday Life* is very relevant here). So Madame Merle's attitude expresses a deep truth about our society. She has gone the whole way. She is concerned only with the agents of expression — things, clothes, appearances, appurtenances. She reconstructs a false self to show the world. She is what she dresses to be. This is extreme: it entails the death of the soul and the ultimate disappearance of the individual inner self. As Isabel says to herself, it is difficult to imagine Madame Merle 'in any detachment or privacy, she existed only in relations . . . one might wonder what commerce she could possibly hold with her own spirit'. She is rather like Lord Mellifont in "The Private Life" who disappears when he is on his own. If you care only for appearances, you exist only when there are people to look at you.

However, in this key conversation, Isabel's answer to Madame Merle is also extreme. She says: "I know that nothing else expresses me. Nothing that belongs to me is any measure of me; everything's on the contrary a limit, a barrier, and a perfectly arbitrary one . . . . My clothes may express the dressmaker, but they don't express me. To begin with it's not my own choice that I wear them; they're imposed upon me by society". To which Madame Merle wryly answers: "Should you prefer to go without them?"

This is a classic formulation of a basic American attitude. Lionel Trilling once noted that there is something in the American temperament which wishes to resist all conditioning, all actual society, and aspires to a life which will permit the spirit to make its own terms. 'Somewhere in our mental constitution is the demand for life as pure spirit'. (See his essay "William Dean Howells" in *The Opposing Self*). Emerson's 'Self-Reliance', Thoreau by Walden Pond, Whitman celebrating the self — these, of course, are the classic types for the American imagination. They certainly did believe there was such a thing as the 'isolated' self, and welcomed the fact. And characters like Bartleby and Huck Finn and Augie March reveal the ineradicable suspicion of all conditioning forces, all actual fixed social situations. They refuse, opt out, move on. Like Isabel they see barriers and limits everywhere, and much of their energy goes into avoiding the shaping pressures (and appurtenances) of society. Isabel's retort is, thus, in a great American tradition. And up to a point she is right. Things and appurtenances are not identical with the self, as Osmond and Madame Merle make them. We are not what we wear. But to see everything in the actual world as sheer barrier, hindrance, and limit is also dangerous. For without any limits the self can never take on any contours, cannot become something real. The pure spirit of the self has to

involve itself with the material world of things and society in order
to work out an identity for itself, indeed in order to realise itself.
To that extent the self must dress itself and must choose its clothes.
In laying the responsibility for her clothes (i.e. her appearance, her
situation etc.) on society and calling it an arbitrary imposition,
Isabel is being dangerously irresponsible. For it is her error in
thinking that life can be lived as pure spirit in contempt of things
that leads her to mistake Osmond's attitude. The ironic result is
that she puts herself in the power of a man who wants to treat *her*
as a thing. James's insight here is profound. For there is indeed
a dangerously close connection between an idealistic *rejection* of
'things' and an idealising *of* 'things'. This is why Osmond is such a
telling figure. In the appearance of living for the spirit in disregard
of the material, he has in fact simply spiritualised the material.
And James must surely have been one of the first to see into this
particularly modern malaise which other American critics have
mentioned in discussing modern society; namely, the confusion of
the spiritual and material realms, the spiritualising of things. James
knew that things and surroundings (the shell) *were* important:
there was a way of being among things which manifested the
quality of the self, which enabled it to realise itself. But of course
there was also a way of being among things which menaced and
could destroy the self. Isabel Archer's journey is hazardous but
representative: and her error no less than human.

We first see Isabel — as we last see her — in a garden. This is
always an important setting in James (usually indicating a place of
meditation and appreciation). Gardens are certainly important in
this book. At the start of her European journey Isabel regards her
inner world as a garden and indeed many of her happiest moments
are spent in them. She is happiest, in particular, at Gardencourt,
and the very name points to the fact that this is the locale in the
book which most exudes a mood of mellow reciprocity between the
civilised and the natural. But Isabel is far from appreciating it at
the start of her adventures. She sees it only as romantic and
picturesque. It is only much later that she appreciates that it is
something more real and indeed more sacred than that. After this
opening glimpse James takes us back to the house in Albany, New
England, where Isabel started on her travels. The most important
of many suggestive details about this house is the 'condemned door',
the entrance which 'was secured by bolts which a particularly
slender little girl found it impossible to slide'. It is to be Isabel's
later fate again to be locked in. Also, the windows are covered, but

'she had no wish to look out, for this would have interfered with her theory that there was a strange, unseen place on the other side — a place which became to the child's imagination, according to different moods, a region of delight or terror'. This of course expresses Isabel's whole attitude to life: her theories and imagined versions of reality are generated behind closed doors and covered windows. Instead of venturing forth she sits poring over books. One more detail is particularly prophetic: she 'had the whole house to choose from, and the room she had selected was the most depressed of its scenes'. James often used the metaphor 'the house of life' and indeed, of its many rooms, Isabel is yet to choose the darkest and most imprisoning.

If you see Isabel's quest as being at least in part a search for the right house then her reactions to Warburton and Osmond become even more revealing. When she rejects Warburton after visting his house, Lockleigh, she puts her rejection in this way: she says she is unable "to think of your home . . . as the settled seat of my existence". As though the main thing about him was the fact that he doesn't have what she regards as the right house. Osmond's house is brilliantly described. First of all, it is on a hill-top, the best place for a person who wants to put the claims of the base world behind and live a life of ideal appreciation and detached observation. Clearly Isabel is attracted to this degree of rarefied removal. But we note that in the first, perfectly plausible, topographical description, the front of the house is deceptive. 'It was the mask, not the face of the house. It had heavy lids, but no eyes; the house in reality looked another way . . . .' This, I need hardly point out, is entirely true of its owner. Even the windows bespeak Osmond: 'their function seemed less to offer communication with the world than to defy the world to look in'. Isabel's approach to this key dwelling is laced with subtle portent, and I must quote at some length here. 'The companions drove out of the Roman Gate . . . and wound between high-walled lanes into which the wealth of blossoming orchards overdrooped and flung a fragrance, until they reached the small suburban piazza, of crooked shape, where the long brown wall of the villa occupied by Mr. Osmond formed a principal, or at least very imposing, object'. They drive into the courtyard. 'There was something grave and strong in the place; it looked somehow as if, once you were in, you would need an act of energy to get out. For Isabel, however, there was of course as yet no thought of getting out, but only of advancing'. The whole drive provides a compressed analogue for Isabel's venture into life so far. The blooming promising beginning, the flung fragrance (Touchett's unlooked-for bequest perhaps), then the crooked square, the preventing wall, and the enclosing courtyard — the whole passage subtly prepares us for what becomes explicit only much later when Isabel realises that 'she had taken all the first steps in the purest confidence, and then she had suddenly found the infinite vistas of a multiplied life to be a dark, narrow alley with a dead wall at the end'. And note the geography of the following image. 'Instead of leading to the high places of happiness, from which the world would seem to lie below one, so that one could look down with a sense of exaltation and advantage, and judge and choose and pity, it led rather downward and earthward, into the realms of restriction and depression where the sound of other lives, easier and freer, was heard as from above, and where it served to deepen the feeling of failure'. Isabel thinks Osmond lives on the heights of meditation and free appreciation, but really he dwells in the depths of calculation and constricting appropriation. Her life seemed to lead up to the world of ends; instead she was plunging down into the world of means. Osmond's palace of art turns out to be 'the house of darkness, the house of dumbness, the house of suffocation'. But it was the house she chose. James knits his imagery together in the famous description of Isabel's reaction when Osmond proposes. She feels 'a pang that suggested to her somehow the slipping of a fine bolt — backward, forward, she couldn't have said which'. Is she about to be released or immured? In her most testing moment she is unable to distinguish what presages liberation and expansion, and what threatens detainment and constriction. Her radical confusion is all there in the image.

I will not here describe the many galleries and museums and other houses and rooms Isabel passes through, but all repay careful study. For in this book all the architecture means something of specific importance to Isabel, as of course it must to the self seeking both freedom *and* form. Pansy's convent, for instance, has all the appearance of a prison to Isabel's clearer vision. On the other hand, some architecture can offer consolation. For example there is a beautiful passage describing a ride she takes in Rome — 'the place where people had suffered' — some time after her discovery of the truth about Osmond. 'She had long before taken old Rome into her confidence, for in a world of ruins the ruin of her happiness seemed a less unnatural catastrophe. She rested her weariness upon things that had crumbled for centuries and yet were still upright: she dropped her secret sadness into the silence of lonely places'. It is a most moving description of the bruised and erring spirit absorbing strengthening reminders and consoling clues from the marred but splendid debris of human habitations of the past. And one of the reasons why Isabel returns to Rome at the end, renouncing the refuge of Gardencourt which she now does appreciate as sacred, is that the self has to return to the place where it made its most defining, if mistaken, choice. That is where the work of re-habilitation and re-education must go on. It is where knowledge is earned. I think this is why, in the last scene of the book, we see Isabel running from the darkening garden of meditation back into the well-lit house of life. But before exploring that decision I want to discuss the significance of Ralph.

IV

Ralph is of course a recurring Jamesian figure — the subtly debarred spectator who enjoys everything in imagination and nothing in action. Thus Ralph has 'the imagination of loving' but has 'forbidden himself the riot of expression'. All his happiness consists of 'the sweet-tasting property of the observed thing in itself'. To appreciate the 'thing in itself' is precisely to be an inhabitant of the world of ends. Ralph is wise, he is dying: 'restricted to mere spectatorship at the game of life', banned from participation, addicted to appreciation. A true Jamesian artist figure. Suitably, he is most often seen sitting in gardens. On one occasion in particular the contrast between 'house' and 'garden' is used to good effect. This is when Ralph tells Isabel the real truth about Osmond. She, with her theories, rejects his visions — and leaves the garden. She ends the conversation 'by turning away and walking back to the house'. But Ralph cannot follow her: it is too cold for him in the house, he is too susceptible to 'the lurking chill of the high-walled court'. It does not seem to me excessive to see Ralph as the artist-meditator, who cannot function in the house of life but who indulges his imagination and speculation in the garden. He sits; he does not act. He is content to watch and appreciate Isabel; he has no thought of dominating or manipulating her. In his own way he is also an aesthete, someone who stands back and relishes the beautiful. But where Osmond is a false aesthete, Ralph has the true artistic instincts. Osmond wants to turn Isabel into a work of art (we see her at his home 'framed in the gilded doorway' already adjusting to her status as portrait); Ralph appreciates her living qualities artistically. Osmond hates Ralph because he is 'an apostle of freedom'. But as Isabel comes to see, Ralph is more intelligent, more just, better. Not egotistic, as Osmond always is. This leads up to the deathbed scene. Isabel is back at Gardencourt, happy at least that she is no longer having to act and falsify. At Gardencourt she can be her self, her true self. And, dying, Ralph comforts her: "But love remains". He tells her she has been adored and her response is revealingly simple. "Oh my brother". In Osmond Isabel thought she recognised a soul mate. She was very wrong. At last, having suffered, she realises who is the true image of what her self wants to be — Ralph. "Oh my brother." Having seen through the false aesthetic approach to life, she now appreciates the true artistic attitude: a vision based on love, on generosity, on respect for things in themselves and a gift of unselfish appreciation.

In taking the measure of Osmond, Isabel has started to move towards Ralph's point of view. The great chapter, forty-two, when she takes stock, is really the beginning of her deeper knowledge and clear vision. She is starting to read things properly, as Ralph does. And with this new access of vision, Isabel becomes less active externally and more active internally. She has started on what James later called 'the subjective adventure': the adventure of trying to understand, to sound out depths, to appreciate qualities, to transcend the importunities of the ego. By the end of the book Isabel Archer has started to become a Jamesian artist.

Just before the end we see her in the garden at Gardencourt: this time pensive and quiet, much closer to a knowledge of true values than when we saw her stride so confidently on to that lawn at the start. It is now twilight: she is sitting on a bench alone. This stance, this setting, becomes a dominant one in James's later work — not only in the last great story "The Bench of Desolation" but in such works as *The Ambassadors* as well as in many stories like "Crapy Cornelia" and "Mora Montravers". In that last story, for instance, we see the self-effacing Traffle, excluded, estranged, sitting staring at the approaching evening with only one consolation. As the night comes down on him he has, for company, his Jamesian mind: 'exquisite, occult, dangerous and sacred, to which everything ministered and which nothing could take away.' Clearly James had a recurring vision of a person who has somehow failed to realise him (or her) self in the physical world, who has renounced all active participation, and who withdraws into sedentary isolation consoling himself with the fruits of a finer, if sadder, consciousness. Isabel, we feel, is drawing towards her truer role as she sits in the darkening garden. But she is interrupted by Caspar Goodwood, who comes to disturb her on her bench in the garden: she cannot yet enjoy Ralph's invalid immunity from the challenge and threat of engagement. Goodwood kisses her, and in a curious cluster of images James implies that she is both wrecked and then freed. Goodwood brings a possessive lightning, 'but when darkness returned she was free'. I am not fully certain of James's intention here, but the effect is this. For a long time she has wondered if her true fate, the true realisation of her self, should not have been with Goodwood. Now for the first time she is subjected to the full force of his sexual claims. It is a shattering experience, but it is also a release. She was not made to go that way. There is no going back to the simple level of life he represents. He tries to prevent her from returning to Rome where, as he says, she has to 'play a part' and maintain a false 'form': but it is precisely this that she must, at this stage, do. She runs back to the house: 'there were lights in the window of the house; they shone far across the lawn'. She reaches the door. 'Here only she paused. She looked all about her; she listened a little; then she put her hand on the latch. She had not known where to turn; but she knew now. There was a very straight path'. James has annoyed readers by not saying what that path is. But I think the wonderful suggestivity of this last scene tells us all we need. The last pause and lingering look surely imply that she is reluctant to leave the garden — a refuge and a place of meditation. But she cannot opt out of her fate so easily, just as even more she cannot return to American innocence and physical simplicity with Goodwood. She chose her room in the house of life and she must return to it. She must return to the chill and ruins of Rome: for the self cannot back out of a mistaken course but only push through and move beyond. But she takes back with her a new vision, a deeper understanding, a capacity for modest unegotistical contemplation which all promise a richer future — a future in which she will come to a true realisation of what her real self is. It is beside the point to ask whether she will divorce Osmond. When she has attained her new vision, he simply shrinks into insignificance, just as Madame Merle melts away to America. We do not even hear his voice for the last seventy pages or so of the book, and by the end of the book we feel that Isabel has attained the most important kind of freedom, an internal one. She is liberated from her twisted vision and her confused values. She can see through all false appearances. She returns to Italy, to the 'ruins' she herself was partly responsible for. But she will not, we feel, ever again be subordinate to the deceptions and calculations of a worldling like

Osmond. Even if she does not break out of the house and kick over
the traces, and even if she never again indulges in any more
passions, her future will be quite other. For her way of looking has
changed. Now I think one might fairly suggest that James, in fact,
could not see exactly what sort of future such a person might have,
how she might take up her place again in the social scene. We can
admire Isabel's fine stoicism and admit at the same time that it is
hard to visualise the details of her future. And this, I think, is
because James is already feeling the necessary connection between
the artistic observation of life *and* the renunciation of active participation in it. As Isabel becomes more the artist, in her mind, so
she will withdraw from social involvement, if not physically then at
least psychologically. If she never returns to sit in the garden of
Gardencourt, then we may be sure she will spend many later years
reposing in the garden of her mind. With James's later artist figures
or observers, the attempt at any active participation is all but
abandoned from the start. Hyacinth Robinson[2] finds no satisfying
role or niche for himself in society and shoots himself. Lambert
Strether[3] develops a new complex comprehensiveness of vision and
appreciation, but to retain it, it is essential that he must not get
'anything for myself' — no spoils, no physical relationships. The
narrator of *The Sacred Fount* is the conscience of society, at the
cost of never enjoying its actual embrace. There are other such
figures, but none perhaps so humanly comprehensible as Isabel
Archer, in whom we can see the erring self emerging into the
incipient artist. With later characters the divorce between action
and observation is almost accepted as inevitable from the start.
It would seem that James, in his own way, came to share Goethe's
reflection that 'the acting man is always without conscience; no
one has conscience but the observing man'. If nothing else, *The
Portrait of a Lady* shows us the birth of a conscience out of the
spoiling of a life.

----

[2] [The hero of *The Princess Casamassima* (1886). — EDITOR.]
[3] [The hero of *The Ambassadors* (1903). — EDITOR.]